Roses

A CONCISE GUIDE IN COLOUR

Roses

by Ludvík Večeřa

Illustrated by

Jiřina Kaplická

Hamlyn

London   New York   Sydney   Toronto

Translated by Olga Kuthanová
Designed and produced by Artia for
The Hamlyn Publishing Group Limited
London New York Sydney Toronto
Hamlyn House, Feltham, Middlesex,
England
Copyright © Artia 1971
Reprinted 1973

ISBN 0 600 31635 1

Printed in Czechoslovakia

CONTENTS

THE HISTORY AND GEOGRAPHICAL DISTRIBUTION OF ROSES

Information on the history of roses is gleaned from the data amassed by archaeologists in their investigations of ancient and vanished civilizations. Thanks to the efforts of Sir Leonard Woolley, it is known that about 5,000 years ago the Sumerian King Sargon I lived in the city of Ur lying between the Euphrates and Tigris rivers, and that he brought home roses from his military compaigns in the land now known as Turkey. The records discovered by Woolley are the oldest to date, but in view of the fact that Man has existed for about 1,000,000 years the information about roses left by the Sumerians is relatively very recent. Moreover, if Sargon I was able to introduce roses to his land they must have grown elsewhere long before that. And this is found to be true. Scientists have discovered that roses grew and flowered a long time before, and in many instances have evidence that they were in being even as early as the Tertiary. In their work these scientists deal with finds of prehistoric roses and attempt to prove that roses were present on the earth as far back as 25,000,000 years at the least, a time when there was as yet no sign of Man. The existence of roses in the Tertiary is borne out by fossils; imprints of parts of leaves, shoots and thorns and even one imprint of a bud have been found.

According to Blassau, certain fossil species can be compared to those of the present day:

Fossil species	Site	Similar present-day species
R. akashiensis	Japan	R. roxburghii TRATT.
R. polyantha	Japan	R. multiflora THUNB.
R. Hoerneri	China-Kansu	R. acicularis LINDL.
R. shanwangensis	Japan	R. rugosa THUNB.

On the basis of these discoveries it can be assumed that the territories where these remains of prehistoric roses were found have been uninterruptedly populated by roses for about 25,000,000 years and that most probably Asia is the cradle of these lovely flowers. The history of roses is therefore much older than the history of the human race.

The majority of present-day species are to be found in the temperate zone of the Northern Hemisphere; only very few grow in the areas to the north and south. One exception is *R. acicularis* LINDL. which, because of its hardiness in low temperatures, has made its way round the whole polar circle over a period of millions of years. Another exception is *R. montezumae* HUMB. and BOMPL. which, unlike *R. acicularis*, grows in subtropical Mexico. Similar exceptions are the species growing in the subtropical regions on the coasts of Europe and Africa bordering the Mediterranean. These are primarily *R. corymbifera* BORKH., *R. montana* CAI., *R. pouzonii* TRATT., *R. serafinii* VIV. and *R. sicula* TRATT.

ROSES IN THE HISTORY OF NATIONS

Periods in the history of mankind denoted by historians as periods of wealth and prosperity have always been marked by roses and the same is also true of the present day. The rose has often played an important role in religion, literature, politics and economics. The influence of the rose on economics, in this case detrimental, was referred to by Horace more than 2,000 years ago when he complained of the conditions in the Roman Empire, stating that grain fields and fruit orchards were planted with roses. This indicates that the cultivation of roses was probably more profitable than the growing of food crops in the Rome of that era. The same is true in many countries today. In about 600 B.C., the Greek poetess Sappho, who is said to have been the first to call the rose the queen of flowers, enshrined it in one of the fragments of her lyrical poems which has survived. Queen it was and queen it has remained unto this day.

THE ANCIENT WORLD

As has already been stated, the oldest written records were discovered in the royal tombs in Ur. However, for several centuries following the era of King Sargon I (2684—2630 B.C.) there are no further records and therefore it can only be surmised that the rose was introduced from this region to Crete and Greece and from there via the rivers of Babylon and along the trade routes by caravan to Egypt and North Africa. From wall paintings which have been preserved and pictures on clay vessels unearthed during archaeological excavations in the Palace of Knossos on Crete, it seems that the existence and popularity of roses were already established in the mid-Minoan period (by about 1600 B.C.). Nothing specific is known of roses in Egypt at a similar date. The garland of nine roses discovered by archaeologists in an Egyptian tomb in 1888 probably dates from sometime between the fifth and third centuries B.C. It may be some form of the French Rose (*Rosa gallica*) which the Romans later called *R. sancta*. In the *Avesta*, the holy scripture of the Persians, the rose appears as a religious symbol for the first time in history. Fragmentary records about the cult of the rose were also found in India and Syria.

In the thousand-year-old Chinese Empire the rose was a highly esteemed flower. From reports by the famous philosopher Kung-fu-tse (551—479 B.C.) it is known that in his day the imperial library contained 600 books on roses. Attar of roses was already being produced in China at that time. Its use, however, was restricted to the privileged few. The common people were allowed to wear on their bodies only a pouch containing a few dried rose petals, which was regarded as a protection against evil spirits.

The cultivation of roses was a highly esteemed and successful business but the results of the work of Chinese growers did not become known in Europe until 1789. The great influence of the Chinese rose on the evolution of roses throughout the world is discussed later.

A coin, dating from circa 80 B.C. and bearing a six-petalled rose, was found on the island of Rhodes. Roses in Cretan paintings also have the same number of petals. The reason why artists of that time painted roses with six petals, which is incorrect botanically, is not known.

Homer, who lived in about 900 B.C., writes that Achilles' shield was decorated with roses and that Aphrodite anointed Hector's dead body with an ointment made from roses. The rose was consecrated to Aphrodite, the Greek goddess of love and beauty, and later to the Roman Venus. The Greek poet Anacreon (580—495 B.C.) often sings the praises of the rose, relating how it grew from the white sea foam whence Aphrodite, the goddess of love, emerged. One of the many legends about the rose tells that the Corinthian Queen Rhodanthe transformed herself into a rose when she wearied of the attentions of her many suitors.

Although Herodotus, who died in about 425 B.C., lived long in Athens he was born on the shores of Asia Minor. He knew his native land well and believed that it was Midas, King of Phrygia, who introduced the rose to Macedonia from Asia Minor in about 700 B.C. (ancient Phrygia included a large part of present-day Turkey). Herodotus also writes of roses with sixty petals. The first real descriptions of roses, however, date from the time of Theophrastus (372—287 B.C.) who describes roses with five, fifteen, twenty and a hundred petals. He also wrote of the propagation of roses by cuttings which he considered better than those from seed, for such roses flower sooner.

Roses were cultivated throughout the whole of ancient

Hellas. Greek colonizers could easily have introduced them to Sicily and Africa. Roses found their way from the Appenine Peninsula to the Pyrenees, from there to France and, perhaps only slightly later, also to England.

Similarly in the Roman Empire roses were known long before the Christian era. Pliny the Elder (A.D. 23—79) writes of them in detail and like Theophrastus before him he, too, speaks of a rose with a hundred petals, probably a form of the French Rose *(R. gallica)*. However, it may have been the Musk Rose *(R. moschata)* or even the Evergreen Rose *(R. sempervirens)*.

The Romans prized the rose above all other flowers and used it to adorn not only their homes but also their beds and baths, where it served a more utilitarian purpose, for rose blossoms in the bath water were supposed to preserve a woman's youth and beauty. Rose petals put on the face for the night smoothed out wrinkles. The quantities of roses required for feasts were enormous and so large rose plantations sprang up not only in Italy but also in the warmer climate of Egypt. Rose petals were shipped to Rome by boat, rather a costly venture to say the least, and it is said that Nero paid a ton of gold for one such shipment.

The Romans knew how to bud roses and also how to force their growth so that they bloomed by the end of winter. These 'winter' roses *(Rosae hibernae)* were considered a gardening triumph and were cultivated in great numbers, so great, in fact, that in time it was possible to do without imports from Egypt.

Towards the end of the Roman era there were increasingly fewer wealthy citizens and consequently fewer means for the costly cultivation of roses. Only the hardiest roses survived the fall of the Roman Empire and most of them became wild.

THE MIDDLE AGES

At some point during the rise of Christianity the rose was rejected, for it was too strong a reminder of the cruelty of pagan days. All pagan customs were similarly rejected, especially gifts of flowers, which the heathen placed in the graves of the dead. It was not until centuries later that the Roman Catholic Church changed its attitude and the red rose was adopted as the symbol of Christ's blood. Records from the year 1049 mention for the first time that Pope Leo IX conferred the 'Golden Rose' on women of virtue via his ambassadors. The Golden Rose was an ornament consisting of a branch with petals of gold filled with musk and balsam. On various occasions in later years it was conferred on high church and state officials and on religious organizations.

In thirteenth-century France the quantity of roses used to make wreaths was so great that it gave rise to a new trade: the cut-flower trade. Florists were allowed to work even on Sundays. At that time the rose was considered to be a messenger from heaven to children on earth and was supposed to bring God's blessing; this was the reason why it was recommended that churches should be built near to places where roses grew. The site for the cathedral at Hildesheim was selected by this means, and it is said that the original rose bush *R. canina* L. still grows by the church wall. Comparatively recently, the late priest Seebald presented a treatise which, on the basis of reliable findings, is supposed to prove that this huge bush is at least 500 years old, though the possibility of its being 1,000 years old cannot be excluded. The reinstatement of the rose in the Christian world is similarly borne out by the fact that rose water was used to fill the holy water stoops on important church feasts. And not just the church but knights and troubadours as well sang the praises of the rose as the symbol of love — earthly love as opposed to that of the church.

SUPERSTITIONS AND LEGENDS
ABOUT ROSES

Market gardeners in certain countries are well acquainted with the aversion of customers to cut yellow roses, for these are believed to be the symbol of perfidy. What gave rise to this belief? It is said that while Mohammed was away fighting the Israelites in the year 612 his favourite wife Aisha passed her time in the company of a certain young Persian. Upon his return from the wars Mohammed was not fully convinced of Aisha's faithfulness and wished to make sure. He therefore bade her immerse a branch of red roses in the palace well. If the blooms did not change colour he would be satisfied. Aisha is said to have done as she was told, but to her great surprise when she pulled the blooms out they were a lovely saffron yellow.

A tenth-century legend tells that all the roses in paradise were white as lilies, but that they turned red with shame after Eve had sinned. Today we know that lilies may be red and roses white, one of the popular cultivars even bearing the exemplary name 'Virgo' (virgin). If one were to look for a logical explanation for the rise of this legend then perhaps it is the fact that the author of the tale knew only the French *(R. gallica)* and Damask *(R. damascena)* roses with red blooms, or that Eve's sin was not so terrible and Mother Nature shut her eye to it and left some white roses for our pleasure as well.

The rose, however, as everyone knows, was not only a symbol of love. The year 1455 marked the beginning of the conflict between the Houses of York and Lancaster. The York coat-of-arms contained a white rose, perhaps *R. alba incarnata*, whereas that of the House of Lancaster had a red rose, copied perhaps — if the designer of the heraldic emblem looked to cultivated roses as his inspiration — from the French rose 'Red Damask'. The dispute between the two houses grew into the Wars of the Roses, the real stake being the crown of England to which each family laid claim. Following the end of the war the rose, symbolizing the reconciliation of the two houses, was depicted on the coins of the realm together with the portrait of Henry VII, King of England. It is said that the reconciliation was also brought about in part by the gardener Miellez, in that he cross-bred the two roses, the outcome being a red and white striped rose *R. damascena versicolor*, called the York and Lancaster Rose.

Medicinal and beauty preparations made from the petals of the rose have been known since ancient times but it was not until the mid-seventeenth century that attempts to produce attar of roses in Europe were crowned with success. This oil was used in the treatment of eye diseases, a common belief being that when applied round the eyes it strengthened the eyesight and eradicated pain. Besides attar of roses and rose water the herbalists also made rose honey and rose vinegar and preserved rose petals. The jars contained a mixture of ground petals mixed with sugar, highly recommended also for the treatment of liver disorders and diseases caused by fungi. Attar of roses in addition to its many other uses was supposed to cure nosebleeds, and to relieve headaches and heartburn. Rose sugar cured consumption. Smoke from dried rose petals placed on glowing charcoal helped alleviate stabbing pains in the ear.

For the mediaeval maiden the rose had still other, more attractive properties. Thus, for instance, she could win the youth she desired by wearing a white, red and pink rose over her heart for three days in succession. These roses were then soaked in wine for another three days and all that remained was to give the resulting brew to the chosen 'victim' and his fate was sealed.

ROSE GARDENS AND ROSARIA

The first known rose garden was laid out by King Childebert (d. A.D. 558) in Paris for his wife. Surviving records reveal that the cultivation of roses in France dates from the year 800. It is known that they were ordered to be grown in the castles and palaces but it is not certain whether it was Charles the Great or his son who issued this decree.

Monasteries were the main rose propagators and growers and it has been proved that this was how the southern European roses found their way to Scandinavia in the middle of the twelfth century.

In the following centuries roses were also brought to central and northern Europe by the crusaders and thus *R. damascena* was again brought directly from Damascus.

In the sixteenth century it became the fashion to build rosaria, collections of rose species brought together for their botanical interest. These were, however, more a collection of curiosities than a decorative feature. Collectors of the Renaissance pursued neither scientific nor business aims in their gardens, but it is thanks to them that many interesting roses came to grace the gardens of Europe. Thus, for instance, in 1580 the yellow *R. lutea*, its various races being grouped today under the species *R. foetida*, was brought here from Asia Minor. The red and white *R. foetida (R. lutea bicolor)* is a great favourite to this day. Another important rose dating from this time is *R. moschata* (Musk Rose), brought from the Himalayas. Holland was the European centre of rose cultivation in the late sixteenth and early seventeenth centuries. It was here that the mutation *R. centifolia muscosa* (Moss Rose) first made its appearance. Renaissance roses are admired to this day in the paintings of Raphael, Michelangelo, Leonardo da Vinci and Boticelli. The Dutch painter Jan Breughel the Elder loved roses so much that he was called the 'flower' Breughel.

The Baroque did not have a great feeling for the rose. Gardens predominantly comprised ground-cover plantings of flowers and box trees trimmed into various shapes. Besides, the eighteenth-century roses, with their comparatively little decorative foliage and fairly brief flowering period, only rarely repeated, could not vie with the attractive new flowers such as dahlias, narcissi and peonies brought from overseas.

An important date in the history of the rose is the year 1804, when at the behest of the Empress Josephine, wife of Napoleon I, the gardeners Dupont and Hardy began to establish extensive rose gardens at Malmaison. It was a full twenty-five years before the rosaria were completed in their entirety. The Empress lived here only until 1814 but during this time she acquired all the important roses of her day and thus made possible the beginning of significant cultivating efforts which greatly influenced further evolution in this field.

In the eighteenth century it was still possible to have all the species and varieties of roses then known in Europe in a single rosarium. Leaving aside the conditions of shipment and speed of delivery of those days, this was not too difficult a task, for at that time there were only about 200 to 300 known species and varieties, about the number that is currently cultivated by any of the larger modern nurseries. Today it would be impossible, even from the purely technical and economic viewpoints, to keep in good order a rosarium comprising the more than 20,000 species and varieties that are known to present-day rose growers and collectors. Cultivating and keeping a large collection was attempted by many rosaria in various countries for decades. Towards the end of summer, however, rose collections of such vastness tend to dissuade rose lovers rather than win them over to this fascinating pastime. This is quite understandable, for all species and varieties do not thrive in the climate and soil of a single location. Under such conditions even the greatest care will not ward off serious fungus diseases of the leaves,

amage by frost, etc. The larger the collection the more often
re there empty spaces in the bed or roses without foliage.
howing, and thereby recommending only those blooms that
re considered the best and most valuable from the grower's
iewpoint, is becoming increasingly widespread and large
osaria incorporating a wide range of species and varieties
re being replaced by rose gardens where the queen of flowers
s presented at her best and loveliest. The measure of the
mportance of a modern rose garden is not in the number of
arieties it contains, but in the quality of the selected roses
nd their use in the landscape scheme. The function of the
osaria of the past has been taken over by variety testing
tations, where the planted varieties are not only observed
ut also evaluated and the unsuitable ones eliminated from
urther cultivation. The Royal National Rose Society has its
wn trial grounds near St. Albans, Hertfordshire.

The rose garden has a place for roses of all types. Nevertheless the rose, although it will inevitably be its chief ornament, should not be all pervading. It should be supplemented
by suitable deciduous shrubs and evergreens, keeping the
scene attractive even when the roses are not in bloom during
the spring and winter. Rose gardens are being planted all
over Europe and the selection of species and varieties is
naturally adapted to the local conditions of the given site.

THE GENUS *ROSA* L. – THE ROSE

The classification of plants belongs to the sphere of systematic
botany which classes plants according to their mutual rela-
tionship (according to the origin of the type) into a natural
phylogenetic system that corresponds to our present-day
knowledge of nature's evolution. The best artificial system
was established by the Swedish botanist Carl Linnaeus

17

(1707—1778) who classified and described the then known plants according to the external characteristics of the reproductive organs in the flowers. He was the first to designate plants by a generic and specific name and thus became the father of the now internationally valid binomial nomenclature. According to the rules of nomenclature this binomial designation is followed by the name, initials or abbreviated name of the person who made the first scientific description.

The common wild rose, or Dog Rose as it is called in some countries, is designated since Linnaeus' day under the generic name *Rosa* and specific name *canina* (derived from the Latin word *canis*, meaning dog) followed by the author's initial L. for Linnaeus. The entire botanical name is therefore, *Rosa canina* L.

The genus *Rosa* L. has an exceptional wealth of species and is thus very complicated. The botanical characteristics of the genus *Rosa* L. are more or less the same in the various botanical publications, but opinions as to the classification into species differ. A way out of this difficulty was found by the Belgian botanist Crépin (1830—1903) who created a very practical system of classification according to which it would be possible to class all wild roses into subgroups or sections on the basis of precisely determined external (morphological) characteristics. For every section — sixteen in all — Crépin chose a certain type, a sort of standard, to which he ranged those roses whose individual characteristics showed the greatest resemblance to the given type. Thus, for instance, *Rosa canina* L., the Dog Rose, was the type plant for the section Caninae. The number of species in the various sections is not the same. This type of classification is only used for species roses, not for cultivars (cultivated varieties which are given fanciful names, such as 'Peace').

18

ITEMS OF INTEREST ABOUT THORNS, STEMS, FLOWERS, HIPS AND SEEDS

One of the typical characteristics of the rose is its thorns. However, according to precise botanical terminology the thorns of a rose are not really thorns but spines. A thorn is a modified branch ending in a sharply pointed structure, as seen in Blackthorn *(Prunus spinosa* L.*)*, bearing on it flower buds and small leaves like any other branch, and being continuous with the woody structure of the main stem. Spines are superficial outgrowths of the skin or epidermis. They too are sharply pointed but are often green or tinged with red and the basal cells become flat and corky. Their removal does not cause tearing of the stem but is easy, leaving an oval healed scar. In horticulture, however, 'spines', 'thorns' and 'prickles' (leaf spines formed along leaf margins) seem to be very muddled terms. Roses are characterized by the possession of spines situated on the stems, leaf stalks and undersides of leaf veins, but these are often called thorns; for example the variety 'Zephirine Drouhin' is often described as the thornless rose or rose without a thorn. Easy removal of the spines from the shoots is an important characteristic required of rose varieties cultivated for the cut flowers.

The stem is another part of the rose plant that is of importance for the grower. This is the one-year, more or less woody part of the shoot between the flower and older wood. The upper part of the stem, between the flower and the last leaf, is leafless and is called the neck. The characteristics of the neck, namely its flexibility, firmness and length, are important criteria for judging the value of varieties grown especially for the cut flowers. Flowers may be single, semi-double or double depending on the number of petals. Buds may be of the kind found in the large-flowered varieties — long and pointed, opening into high-centred blooms — or those of the flat, low-centred blooms most commonly found

19

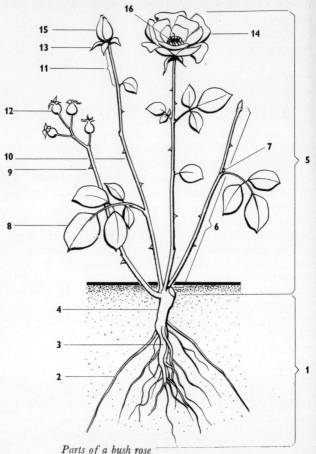

Parts of a bush rose
1 — *rootstock*, 2 — *branch root*, 3 — *main root*, 4 — *root neck*, 5 — *grafted cultivar*, 6 — *one-year shoot*, 7 — *bud (eye)*, 8 — *quinquefoliate leaf*, 9 — *thorn (spine)*, 10 — *stem*, 11 — *neck*, 12 — *hip (hep)*, 13 — *sepals*, 14 — *petals*, 15 — *flower bud*, 16 — *stamens*

in plants flowering in clusters. Abundant or few thorns are considered either an advantage or disadvantage depending on the purpose for which the rose is selected. Roses with few and easily removable thorns are preferred when selecting varieties for the cut flowers. The landscape gardener, on the other hand, may welcome the variety with large, decorative thorns.

The same criterion, that is, the purpose the given rose is to serve, applies in judging the qualities of growth, length of stem, size and character of the flowers, hips and seeds. Hips (sometimes called heps) are fleshy, usually coloured, receptacles enclosing the small hairy fruits of the rose. They remain on the plant after the petals and leaves have dropped and are often of decorative value, varying in size, shape and colour. They are used in the production of rose hip syrup, rich in vitamin C and recommended for young children. Landscape gardeners are interested in roses with hips that are large *(R. rugosa)*, small with attractive sepals *(R. multiflora)*, elongate *(R. moyesii)*, or yellow, red or black. Growers of rootstock are more interested in the number of seeds with good powers of germination contained in the hips, and whether the seeds germinate immediately after they are harvested, as in the case of *R. multiflora*, or whether they must be kept for a time in a mixture of peat and sand (stratification, referred to later in the text).

IMPORTANT STAGES IN THE EVOLUTION OF GARDEN ROSES

Important stages in the evolution of the rose are primarily the periods when its cultivation spread outwards from the cultural centres of the ancient world; at that time the roses cultivated were chiefly the French and Damask roses. The yellow rose *R. foetida* was introduced to Europe from Persia in 1580, and in the early seventeenth century the Dutch produced many new mutations of the Moss rose *(R. centifolia muscosa)*. The first red China or Bengal rose *(R. chinensis)* was brought to France and England in 1789. The famous Noisette was produced in America in 1802 as a cross between *R. moschata* and *R. chinensis* and the first Bourbon rose originated as a cross between the eastern and western roses *R. indica* and *R. damascena* on the Isle de Bourbon in the Indian Ocean. The large-flowered red Bourbon formed the basis for the further evolution of the rose practically up to the present day. Noisettes, Bourbons, Chinas and the resulting tea roses have a repeated flowering period and are therefore known as remontant or perpetuals. The first remontants include the following varieties; 'Josephine Antoinette' (HARDY, 1820), 'Lilacé' (VEILLAND, 1829), 'Madame Audot' (VIBERT, 1825), 'Americaine Belle' (BOLL, 1837), 'La Reine' (LAFFAY, 1842), 'General Jacqueminot' (ROUSSEL, 1853), 'Jules Margottin' (MARGOTTIN, 1853), 'Victor Verdier' (LACHARME, 1859), 'Maréchal Niel' (PRADEL, 1864), 'Fischer et Holmes' (VERDIER, 1865). The variety 'General Jacqueminot' gave rise to the variety 'Ulrich Brunner Fils' (LEVET, 1882) and so on. The first real white rose and one of the most famous perpetuals, 'Frau Karl Druschki' (LAMBERT, 1901), is considered a true hybrid tea by some growers, although 'Madame Caroline Testout' (PERNET DUCHER, 1890) and 'Kaiserin Auguste Viktoria' (LAMBERT, 1891) are generally considered the first. Crossing of the perpetual 'Antoine Ducher' with *R. foetida persiana* REHD. produced the famous yellow variety named 'Soleil d'Or' which gave rise to roses with lovely glossy leaves. Apart from the occasional exception, new hybrid teas are produced by mutual crossing to this day.

The period between the First and Second World Wars was the era of KORDES' gem — 'Crimson Glory' (KORDES, 1935) — followed by the 'rose of roses' — 'Peace' (MEILLAND, 1945),

'Independence' (KORDES, 1951), 'Super Star' (TANTAU, 1960), 'Orange Sensation' (DE RUITER, 1961), and the appearance of new hybridists and new varieties with brilliant new colours such as 'Prélude' (MEILLAND, 1954) and 'Sterling Silver' (FISHER, 1957): a long list indeed of hybrids representing the growers' knowledge, diligence and love of roses.

GARDEN ROSES

It would not be easy to divide the approximately 200 species and several thousand varieties into a few groups that would provide the normal professional or amateur grower with a summary of their most important characteristics. The 'garden' classification of roses is intended to facilitate this task. This system classifies the separate species and varieties into groups either according to typical characteristics evident at first glance or else according to the purpose for which the plant can be used.

The individual groups of the garden classification are as follows:
1. Floribunda roses
2. Hybrid tea roses
3. Miniature roses
4. Climbing roses and ramblers
5. Shrub roses
6. Rootstock roses (wild roses)
7. Species roses

1. FLORIBUNDA ROSES

Floribunda roses are those with flowers grouped into clusters. The oldest of these were developed from *R. multiflora* THUNB., and were produced in France around 1840. They were dwarf bushes with many fragrant but small flowers and were called polyanthas. Their popularity is on the wane as other larger, more attractive forms have been developed. Hybrid polyanthas, now called floribundas, were developed in Denmark in the early 1920s from crosses between polyanthas and large-flowered hybrid tea roses. They included roses suitable for hedges and shrub borders. A third type of these many-flowered roses was developed to combine the best floribundas with the best hybrid tea roses, and these are currently the favourite floribunda roses in cultivation. In America they are called floribunda grandifloras. They are hardy and very colourful and each of the many flowers is perfectly formed. The well-known American authority McFarland therefore does not differentiate polyanthas and hybrid polyanthas from floribundas because, with the passage of time, so many large-flowered varieties have been bred into the floribundas that in some cases it is difficult to decide where to class them. The 'Queen Elizabeth' rose is a typical representative of this group.

2. HYBRID TEA ROSES

These are the second most important group. They are the offspring of noisettes and remontants (perpetuals). Remontants, botanically known as *R. hybrida bifera* (the Latin word *bifera* means twice-flowering), originated as a cross between the Bourbons and China hybrids. Noisettes are themselves hybrids between Musk and China roses. Typical of the hybrid teas are the large, double, high-centred blooms with several other blooms on one stem and above all the exceptionally large colour range — from pure white to dark violet and red with darker shading. True tea roses, known by their tea-like scent, are now rare although they can sometimes be found in old gardens and specialist collections.

3. MINIATURE ROSES

These are small plants with tiny foliage and flowers. The shrubs are not more than 30 cm (12 in) high and the blooms not more than 2.5 cm (1 in) across, hence the name miniature roses. The first known miniature rose, more correctly dwarf China rose, *R. chinensis minima* REHD. *(R. roulettii* CORREVON) was discovered on the island of Mauritius. To this day it has not been proved whether it was the English or the French who brought the first miniature rose to Europe, but that is not important. Far more interesting is that thanks to the Dutch grower Jan de Vinko and also to the Spaniard Pedro Dot and the American Ralph Moore, the first known miniature rose has given us many hybrids so that the number of varieties of widely different colours today runs into dozens. Miniature roses are usually grown in the rock garden, in pots and in the miniature beds of patios and flagstone terraces. The garden classification often shows little respect for the botanical origin of the plant and even groups certain small polyanthas with the miniature China roses.

4. CLIMBING ROSES AND RAMBLERS

This group includes all species and varieties with long shoots which can be tied to supporting frameworks, pillars and walls so that they create the impression of climbing plants. The botanical origins of the individual varieties of climbing roses are not of particular importance in this case for the group embraces a number of various species. Chief of these are *R. arvensis, R. kordesii* WULFF., *R. lambertiana, R. multiflora* THUNB. and *R. wichuraiana* CRÉPIN. Also included in this group are gene mutations of hybrid teas and floribundas with long shoots. One group of climbing roses is called ramblers. Many of these tall, pliable-stemmed plants bearing clusters of small flowers are descended from *R. multiflora* THUNB. and

R. wichuraiana CRÉPIN. The older varieties only bloomed once in the summer but a recently developed form flowers throughout summer and autumn. Ramblers are used to cover fences and pergolas.

5. SHRUB ROSES

Shrub roses are selected types of hybrids derived from rose species which have freely branching stems and variable,

Removal of rootstock shoots (suckers)
1 — rootstock, 2 — grafted cultivar, 3 — rootstock shoot,
4 — leaf of the rootstock rose, 5 — leaf of the cultivar

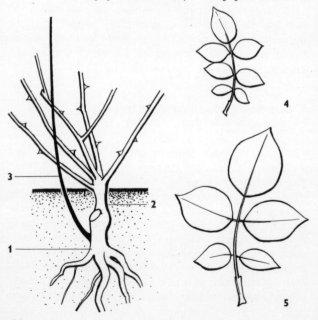

richly scented flowers, some of very beautiful form. Many of the old shrub roses only bloom once in a year but often produce a brilliant display in the autumn with their brightly coloured hips; newer forms are repeat flowering. They are suitable for landscape schemes.

6. ROOTSTOCKS

Rootstocks are wild roses, usually *R. canina* or *R. rugosa*, raised from seed and used to provide a root system on which all other types of roses may be budded. (See section on propagation.) They are sometimes called stocks or under-stocks.

7. SPECIES ROSES

Species roses are the true wild roses. They are noted for hardiness and resistance to disease. Frequently the flowers are single, and are only produced once in a summer.

PROPAGATION OF ROSES

The majority of roses in nurseries are produced by budding the desired variety on to the rootstock of a strong-growing rose. The first stage of cultivation is to provide the rootstocks by gathering hips and sowing seeds or by planting cuttings of rootstock roses which root well. The stock, namely the root and sometimes also part of the stem, used for garden roses is either a true wild rose or one of their simple hybrids.

R. canina inermis is a popular rootstock. It, too, has a vigorous growth and produces shoots with few thorns (*inermis* means thornless), and unlike *R. canina pollmeriana*, another rootstock rose, its shoots are coloured green.

R. coriifolia froebelii (R. dumetorum laxa) is another vigorous rootstock that is moderately thorny and has matt foliage. The red varieties grafted on to this rootstock bear excellent blooms.

R. eglanteria (R. rubiginosa) differs from the preceding stocks by its much slower growth. The shoots are very thorny. It is well suited for a large number of varieties and, because of its slow growth, it has been used more widely in recent years for certain varieties of miniature roses and for cultivation in pots.

R. multiflora has a very vigorous growth continuing well into the autumn months, and is well suited to light soils.

R. indica major, *R. x odorata* and *R. chinensis major* are three synonyms for a rootstock rose with vigorous growth and semi-double, pink, fragrant flowers which has proved eminently suitable especially for the 'Baccara' variety in hothouse cultivation. Unlike other rootstocks it is propagated by cuttings.

PROPAGATION OF ROOTSTOCKS

The cleaned seed of rootstock roses is stored in a mixture of sand and sifted peat. By following this procedure, which gardeners call stratification, they try to imitate the natural process that occurs in the wild and which results in the disintegration of the seed coat so that when sown the seeds germinate at a given time and in as great a number as possible. The length of the stratification period is not the same for all roses. In some types it lasts up to two years but eventually the seedlings produce stems and roots. These plants are used for stocks on to which selected roses may be grafted or budded.

Rootstocks are propagated by special rootstock nurseries whose final product is used for the budding or grafting of selected cultivated varieties. The whole process from the sowing of rootstock seeds to the attainment of a full-grown shrub takes three years for a bush rose and five for a standard.

SOME METHODS OF VEGETATIVE PROPAGATION

The characteristics of the different varieties can be preserved only by vegetative propagation, that is by budding, grafting, cuttings or division. All these methods can be used in the

Methods of vegetative propagation
1 — budding: bud inserted in T-shaped slit on root neck of rootstock, 2 — grafting on to root neck, 3 — root scion

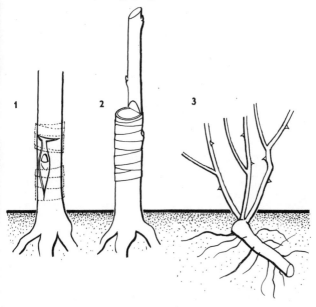

glasshouse, hotbed, or, and this is the most frequent, in the nursery in the open. In commerce the commonest form of propagation is the budding of a latent bud. In this case the growth bud or eye with a small piece of bark, termed the shield, is inserted into a T-shaped slit in the stock in late summer and bound firmly in place with a rubber band. The bud should 'take' in a few weeks but it should not sprout (that is why it is known as a latent bud). The following mid-February the stock above the attached eye is cut off and by autumn the shoot that grows out of the eye will have branched and formed a lovely shrub. Grafting of an active bud is most frequently done under glass in early spring. The bud soon sprouts, and after cutting back (shortening) the young shoots several times the plant will have a nice crown by the end of April so that it can be planted in its permanent site about mid-May, having previously been hardened off by a brief period in a cooler glasshouse. Propagation by division is possible only with roses growing on their own roots (not grafted) such as *R. canina*, *R. gallica* and *R. rugosa*. In the last few years propagation by root cuttings has only been used for *R. nitida* WILLD., excellent for low hedges in large landscape schemes.

Propagation by cuttings, especially 'green' cuttings (that is from grafts during the growth period) is the method most frequently used for miniature roses. The reason for this is that some species of miniature roses produce only very weak, almost filament-like shoots and the grafting of buds on to rootstock requires the skill of a surgeon. With the modern technical equipment of today's propagation glasshouses the propagation of these and other types of roses by means of cuttings not just in summer but practically throughout the year poses no problem. Why, then, do gardeners plant rootstocks, graft buds and perform all these unnecessary tasks when all they need do is put rooted cuttings into plastic bags or containers and sell them during the growth period? The reason budding is preferred to propagation by cuttings is that many roses do not grow well on their own roots, and best results are obtained when they are budded on to selected rootstocks. Less resistant species of cultivated roses propagated by cuttings (own-root roses) may be killed by frost in severe winters, including the roots, but there is a far greater likelihood that when grafted on to rootstock even a severely damaged plant will recuperate and resume growth.

GROWING NEW ROSES

When growing new roses the principal aim should be to improve the characteristics of roses from the viewpoint of man's needs. The chief method used for this purpose is the intentional crossing of two species and the subsequent selection of the best individuals. The first hybrid of such a union is designated *Rosa* x, for instance *Rosa* x *hugoptera*. A more modern method is that of mutational growing where a change in the characteristics occurs spontaneously in a 'sport' or by the influence of chemicals or radio-isotopes on the seeds, whole plants, grafts or cuttings.

HYBRIDIZING

Hybridizing is the combining of the characteristics of two different plants, so-called parents, by fertilization of the female by the male organ.

The actual process of crossing may be carried out in the glasshouse, but is often performed out-of-doors. Flowers of the selected female parent plant are artificially pollinated with pollen from the male parent. The seed is removed from the hip, placed in slightly moist peat moss for a time and then sown in seed boxes in the glasshouse in December or the end of January. The grower must make a daily check of the beds, examine each seedling carefully and immediately discard all those that do not fulfil one or more of the basic requirements. Such a rigid selection, of course, will mean that only a small percentage of the original number of germinated seedlings will reach the final phase, the production of flowers worthy of budding on stock in a nursery.

THE BLUE ROSE

A blue rose is the dream of many growers who would like to augment the colour range of roses. The first, relatively successful attempt to grow a blue hybrid tea was F. Meilland's 'Prélude', produced in 1954. In 1955 Boerner's 'Twilight' made its début and in 1958 Fisher produced his 'Sterling Silver'. Tantau's 'Blue Moon' of 1964 is another valuable variety.

Some of these varieties are distinguished by the lovely form of the flower and unusual, very pleasant fragrance, but in none does the colour begin to match the blue of the Mediterranean or that of alpine gentians. With the exception of the silvery grey-blue 'Sterling Silver', lavender is the prevailing colour in all the varieties mentioned above and often in rather unattractive tints. It is not surprising that there are still many rose lovers who view the efforts to produce a blue rose only as attempts to create a sensation and who do not consider roses of this colour as something worthwhile.

MUTATIONS

Hereditary characters are transmitted by genes. These are complex molecules occurring in chromosomes and arranged in a certain order. Growers attempt to disrupt this order and thus change the hereditary characters by various methods causing mutations. Besides visible changes, such as in colour and growth, there may also be changes that are not evident to the naked eye, changes inside the organism such as greater or lesser resistance to disease and resistance of the flower to the effects of the weather. Mutations may also occur spontaneously, without any intervention on the part of the grower. If the changes involve the whole stem including the flower then the plant is called a 'sport'. There are many such sports, for example 'Madame Butterfly', which is a sport from 'Ophelia'. In recent years greater interest has been shown in intentionally produced artificial — induced — changes in the organism by means of chemicals or irradiation.

EVALUATING NEW ROSES

New varieties of roses, especially ones of a new colour previously unknown in roses or excellent growth traits, are protected by their breeders against unwanted commercial exploitation by means of patents.

The quality of hybrids and mutants is evaluated according to a scoring chart in the form of a scale of points. The various features can receive a score of from zero to nine points according to the official international scale. Traits that are judged are growth, habit, foliage, freedom from disease, character of the shoot and flower stem, form of the bud or formation of the truss, fullness of the flower, period of flowering, perfection of the flower (its ability to shed the petals after they have faded), colour of the opening flower, colour of the full-blown and fading flower, and fragrance.

SELLING ROSES

Today the quality of rose seedlings is determined in all countries by precisely defined rules which are internationally known and accepted. Their observance guarantees not only the authenticity of the given variety but also that it will take and grow well after being planted. The roots of the rose plant are very sensitive to excessive dryness. Lengthy transport and keeping the roses 'heeled in' in the open or in glasshouses sometimes gravely endangers their successful future growth. In this respect much is to be said in favour of the modern methods followed in some countries of keeping the plants in cold storage at a temperature of zero to five degrees centigrade and ninety-eight per cent humidity.

CULTIVATION OF ROSES IN THE GARDEN

THE SITE

The successful cultivation of roses is influenced by many factors, the most important being the climate and nature of the site as regards its exposure (north, south, east, west). Unlike soil, these two are factors that cannot be changed and to which the grower must make the necessary concessions. Success in growing roses in the garden depends principally on the selection of suitable species and varieties — or even rootstock — for the particular climatic conditions, on the layout of the beds and spacing of the individual plants, and on the amount of care given to the plants during the growth period. The following are some of the basic requirements as regards the location.

Roses will only bear a good crop of flowers if they have sufficient light. Thus, for instance, they should not, except for especially selected varieties, be planted on the north wall of a house or on a steep north-facing slope behind it. Positions in almost constant half-shade, such as beneath large spreading trees, are also unsuitable for good growth and flowering. In addition the rose plant has to compete with the roots of these trees which take nourishment from the ground.

In certain climates too much light and especially the hot air alongside the south face of houses and walls may, on hot summer days, cause the blooms of red varieties, which absorb too much sun in such locations, to be literally scorched, but this rarely happens in Great Britain. Roses are also unhappy in situations such as the corners of houses and walls where they are a prey to constant draughts.

As a rule roses will not grow, at least not well, on rocks or in rock fissures, even though one may occasionally find a wild rose growing in such a place. Nor will they thrive in locations that are swampy or excessively damp. There is such a large selection of species and varieties available that it should not be difficult for the gardener to choose the ones best suited to his own soil, situation and climate, from coastal regions to mountain country.

PREPARING THE SOIL

Before starting work it is necessary to make a chemical analysis of the soil nutrients and determine the pH factor, which designates the degree of soil acidity. This analysis should be repeated every five years so that the nutrients can be maintained in the best proportions. Roses do best in slightly acid soil, though they will also grow well in neutral or even decidedly alkaline soils. The optimum pH is between 6 and 7 for both light and heavy soils.

Roses are gross feeders making heavy demands on the soil. A mulch of bulky organic material such as well rotted farmyard manure, spent mushroom compost, or horticultural peat

35

should be placed around a rose plant at ground level to keep the soil moist, improve its structure and provide the essential plantfoods. In sandy soils extra foods are required and these can be added in the form of a proprietary compound fertilizer at 2—4 oz per square yard. Some horticultural firms make up a fertilizer especially for roses. Roses need large amounts of nitrates, phosphates and potash which stimulate good growth and improve disease resistance and promote flowering. They also need smaller quantities of calcium and magnesium to maintain good green colouring of leaves and stems. Very small quantities of iron, boron and manganese are essential for growth. Proprietary fertilizers have in them balanced amounts of these chemicals which are taken up together with water in the soil by the rose roots. Foliar feeding is a novel way of feeding roses through their leaves. Special chemical fertilizers may be diluted in water and sprayed on to the leaves in summer and as a quick tonic to supplement normal feeding.

The actual preparation of the soil consists in double digging it, i.e. digging it to a depth of two spits or spade blades (about 40 cm; 16 in), taking care that the relatively fertile topsoil remains at the top and the subsoil beneath. Well-rotted manure or garden compost should be incorporated with the top spit only. Artificial fertilizers are mixed into the top layer of soil but no later than three weeks before planting.

PLANTING

It is difficult to give precise instructions about the planting distance that should be left between roses as the variation in sizes of named varieties is enormous and, in addition, can vary according to climate. The following table may serve as a rough guide:

Miniature roses	30 cm (12 in)
Hybrid tea and floribunda roses	45 cm (18 in)
Tall-growing and vigorous forms of hybrid tea and floribunda roses	90 cm (3 ft)
Shrub roses for landscaping	180 cm (6 ft)
Climbers	245 cm (8 ft)
Ramblers	300 cm (10 ft)

Planting and pruning after planting
1 — prepared hole, 2 — planted rose and correctly made hollow permitting watering, 3* — hilling up for winter protection, 4* — cutting back the rose in spring after slightly lowering the mound of soil

* applies only in climates with very severe winters

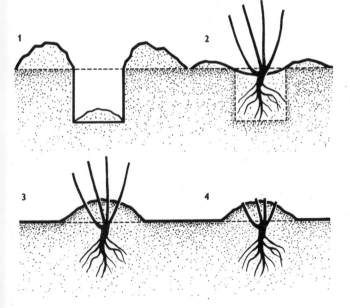

In Britain the best time for planting roses is November (early, if possible) but in very heavy soils it is better to wait until March. The roses should be planted in the following manner:

1. Dig holes 40 cm (16 in) deep and 40 cm (16 in) across and build up a little cone of soil in the bottom.
2. Trim the roots, removing any that are damaged, and cut back the shoots; in autumn planting the reason for trimming the shoots is to ensure that the lengthier ones will not be in the way when the plant is being put in the ground, and to stop the newly planted rose rocking in any high winds.
3. Place the plants in slightly damp earth up to the rootneck.
4. Place the plants in the holes and spread the roots out around the cone of soil at the bottom (the roots of climbing roses should slope away from the wall or trellis against which they are to be trained).
5. Cover the roots with good top soil mixed with compost.
6. Arrange the plant so that the junction of the rootstock and the scion is 3 to 5 cm (1¼ to 2 in) below the general level of the bed and lightly treaddown the soil over the roots.

PRUNING

It is usual to prune established roses in spring. Autumn or winter planted roses are also pruned in spring. Spring planted roses are pruned immediately before planting. Even in Britain climate differences between the northern and southern regions make it necessary to differ the actual time of pruning. In the south, mid-March is usually suitable weather for this operation whereas northern Scotland and mountainous districts of England and Wales experience cold weather in March and pruning is better carried out in April. If pruning takes place too early the newly grown buds will be nipped by frosts; however, if one delays pruning until the sap has begun to rise in the plant, weakening will be caused by loss of sap.

Exceptionally hard pruning results in very vigorous growth. Although this used to be the recommended method, it is now only applied to weak-growing plants to increase their vigour.

The purpose of pruning is to get rid of old wood and promote strong healthy growth. Stems should be cut back to two or three buds from the base using good sharp secateurs

Pruning bush roses: the extent of pruning is marked in black
1 — *hybrid tea*, 2 — *floribunda*, 3 — *miniature*

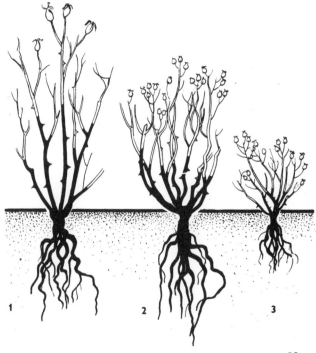

to make a sloping cut 6 mm ($\frac{1}{4}$ in) above an outward-facing lateral bud.

It is difficult to be dogmatic about pruning as growth in different locations differs so much. Established roses usually require lighter pruning than newly planted roses.

In the case of shrub roses for landscape purposes all the very old and weak new shoots are first removed and after that, if it is necessary, the strong, young shoots are lightly trimmed. In pruning these roses it is essential to remember their natural habit of growth and try to prune in accordance with it. Vigorous plants are not cut back as a rule. In order to maintain the shrub in good condition it will suffice to prune the shoots every two or three years.

Ramblers are first of all taken down from their support. All very old shoots (those that can no longer develop new annual growths) are cut out and only about six strong healthy shoots are left. These are lightly trimmed according to need and tied back to the support. Most climbing roses produce the best quality blooms on the laterals growing from the previous year's cane.

Climbing roses are not usually pruned at all, except to remove dead wood, but in order to induce as many new flowering side shoots as possible along the entire length of the cane, it is recommended that the individual canes should be tied in a horizontal to curved line. This is aimed at checking the upward flow of sap which would otherwise promote growth at the tips of the stems only.

The pruning of miniature roses is very simple, requiring only the removal of all dead and damaged shoots and cutting back the remainder to about 5—8 cm ($2—3\frac{1}{4}$ in) above the ground to allow free growth. All the basic rules laid down for their larger counterparts are equally applicable.

Pruning the crowns of tree roses is the same as the pruning of shrub roses except that they are cut back harder.

The general rule to be kept in mind in pruning is that the need of pruning decreases in proportion to increasing growth.

MULCHING

Established roses need not be watered very often as the moisture in the earth can be conserved by mulching. Well-rotted farmyard manure is excellent for this purpose. After clearing the bed the manure is spread out between the bushes so that a layer about 5 cm (2 in) thick covers the whole bed. Prior to levelling the mulch the first half of the required year's dose of artificial feed is scattered between the shrubs. For mulching the manure can be mixed in the ratio of one part manure to one part peat or other suitable material. During the year the mulch can be supplemented with short grass cuttings.

CONTROL OF WEEDS

A mulched surface fosters the growth of roses and limits the growth of annual weeds. Stubborn and long-rooted weeds, however, grow through the mulch and must be destroyed. This can be done either by regular weeding and hoeing, by using chemical agents or a combination of both. Chemical preparations with varied specific effects, the selective weed-killers, are growing in number, and various proprietary brands are obtainable from gardening shops and nurseries. One such preparation used with success is Simazine. This is applied as a spray in the spring while the plant is still dormant. If the application is made at this time it does not matter if parts of the bush are sprayed as well for the active substance is absorbed only by the roots and only by a certain group of plants. Limited in its scope of application is the preparation Paraquat which can be applied as a spray only to the young leaves of weeds. It effectively destroys germinating weeds but unfortunately also harms the foliage of roses and can therefore be used on rose beds only while the plants are dormant. Gramoxon has a short-term effect which

41

commences immediately and leaves the earth without a trace of harmful substances within four hours after application. Developments in the field of chemical weedkillers will undoubtedly make the control of weeds much easier in the near future.

CONTROL OF ROSE PESTS AND DISEASES

In common with all garden plants, roses are subject to attacks by pests and diseases. A well-grown, healthy rose plant can withstand these attacks but a poor specimen, badly·tended, succumbs. If roses are well spaced (not over-crowded), well fed (avoiding over-liming) and obtained from a reputable grower and correctly planted, fear of serious disease is minimal. All cuttings and fallen leaves should be removed from the vicinity of the rose bush and burnt as these harbour eggs of pests, spores and other troubles.

Deficiency diseases are those caused by poor or unbalanced feeding and show in dieback of the shoots, abnormal colouring of the leaves, stunted growth and early leaf fall. Such plants flower poorly or infrequently, with the size, colour and shape of the blooms below average. All can be remedied by the use of a good compound fertilizer. Some firms make these up specially for roses. The directions on the packet should be followed with great accuracy.

Roses may be attacked by animal pests and by fungal diseases. Sometimes weather conditions lead to an abundance of pests and diseases at certain times of the year. Thus an informed and experienced gardener foresees trouble and takes measures to protect his roses and thereby arrests the spread of the parasites.

Insect pests generally breed at a tremendous rate under favourable conditions. Some are winged and fly from plant to plant to spread infection; some are wingless and crawl comparatively short distances feeding voraciously all the time on the soft parts of stems and shoots; others in larval or caterpillar form eat away at leaves doing great damage to the plant. Many are known to carry virus diseases from an infected plant to a previously healthy one.

Most insects at some time in their life cycle are soft-bodied animals and are very easily killed by certain chemicals which are harmless to the plant. The following animals are troublesome to roses:

Aphids (Greenfly) are the commonest rose pests and feed on the sap of the soft new shoots and flower buds. They can be controlled by spraying with a good contact insecticide such as liquid derris or the use of a systemic spray which enters the plant and fights the aphids from the inside and so is not removed by rain.

Capsid bugs cause the leaves to be puckered and distorted and the young buds to wither. These bright green insects can be killed with a systemic spray containing dimethoate or malathion as an active constituent.

Thrips are small, pale-coloured, four-winged insects which attack the flowers causing distortion and dark streaks on the petals. They are most abundant in hot dry weather and are killed by sprays containing nicotine, malathion or menazon.

Sawflies are small caterpillars which cause the leaves to roll, the caterpillar being protected inside the roll, and are hence difficult to reach with sprays. The leaves should be removed and burnt.

Chafer beetle grubs are white, fat grubs about 2.5 cm (1 in) long found in the soil. They gnaw at the roots causing great damage. They should be killed on sight. If the ground is badly infected the top 15 cm (6 in) of soil should be treated chemically prior to planting.

Eelworms are tiny nematodes nearly always present in the soil doing little damage if the soil is kept in good heart.

'Robin's pincushions' are formed by gall wasps and seem to do little damage to the plant.

Frog hopper spit (Cuckoo spit) is frothy white spittle

found on shoots in May. A small insect is protected within the froth and is consequently difficult to reach unless a strong insecticide is used. It causes the leaves and buds to wilt and is worth removal by hand.

Leaf-cutting bees make irregular holes in leaves and though not a serious pest, the result is unsightly.

At the first sign of any rose pests steps must be taken to destroy them before they are able to protect themselves from sprays by hiding away. Early May is usually the time to begin fortnightly spraying with liquid derris or one of the branded rose sprays (systemic chemical insecticides) and repetition of the treatment is recommended as long as the pest is alive.

Many of the newer cultivars of roses are resistant to fungal diseases under normal conditions. However, under epidemic conditions they are certainly not immune. Fungicides are preventatives not cures and should be used before the disease takes a hold, and repeated at intervals as long as the disease condition lasts.

Rose mildew is recognized by powdery white patches on the leaves, stems (even the prickles) and flower buds. This is due to the millions of white spores formed from the fungus which overwinters in the stems. Affected shoots should be cut off and burned. Copper fungicides control the fungus but often damage the leaves, causing scorching. Dinocap will eradicate the disease if used every ten days starting with the very first appearance of trouble.

Black spot appears on roses from April to June and continues until the leaves fall, overwintering on the fallen leaves. Large areas of the leaf are infected. All fallen leaves and prunings should be burned and the trees sprayed with Bordeaux mixture at frequent intervals. Although no roses are immune to black spot, cultivars vary considerably in their susceptibility to the disease. Roses which lack vigour due to poor planting or feeding should be carefully tended with foliar feeding and attention to mulching in dry soils.

Rose rust is not common but fatal, causing orange swellings on the undersides of the leaves. It usually appears in July especially in wet seasons or wetter parts of the British Isles. The orange pustules produce airborne spores which spread the infection. The leaves should be burnt, the cultural conditions improved and the whole plant sprayed with maneb or thiram fortnightly, commencing when the leaves unfold in spring.

Canker is a disease of rose stems and appears as a sunken brown area with swollen edges causing the bark to crack. The infected part should be cut out and burned, cultural conditions should be improved by the application to the soil of a good balanced fertilizer.

It is wise to obtain branded chemicals for control of pests and diseases, and to follow the instructions with great care. Dusting is one method of application in which a fine cloud is produced and each leaf stem or flower thinly coated. Usually it is recommended that dusting should be carried out in the morning while dew is on the plant. Dust guns and powder blowers are used.

Spraying produces fine droplets and is best carried out in the evening and on calm days. Some sprays act directly on the insect but others, called systematic insecticides, enter the sap. They are obviously not washed off by rain. Hand sprays and bucket sprays are suitable for a few rose bushes but hose and diluters are used for larger plots.

SUMMER PRUNING

Pruning during the growth period consists in removing dead flower heads — or whole flower clusters in floribunda varieties — after they have faded. Hard summer pruning, for instance when cutting very long-stemmed blooms of hybrid tea roses for decoration in the home, may weaken the bush. Normally, faded flowers are cut off with three leaves at the most. This mild rejuvenation causes buds to form rapidly in the axils of the remaining leaves thus promoting further flowering. In the case of shrub roses for landscape purposes, as well as floribundas and climbing roses, the flower clusters are cut either at one time or as they die, depending on the variety. Only in the case of varieties or species bearing decorative hips are the flowers left on the plant till they shed their petals themselves. Most hybrid tea and floribunda roses are capable of producing hips and seeds. When this happens the plant no longer produces further flowers and at the end of September such varieties are covered with a quantity of hips instead of blooms, which testifies to insufficient care on the part of the grower.

Summer pruning also includes the removal of young lateral shoots growing from the leaf axils below the main flower of hybrid tea roses. Regular removal of these small shoots that vie with the main bloom for nourishment yields a bloom of outstanding quality.

CALENDAR OF OPERATIONS

The most important operations in the cultivation of roses have their logical sequence which follows the course of the growth period. This is best illustrated by the following schedule:

Operation	Time of execution
Preparation of the soil	January to March
Checking of supports loosened by frosts	October to November
Planting	March to April
	October to mid—December
Winter pruning	mid—February to April
Mulching	mid—February to April

46

Application of artificial feeds	mid—April to May June to mid—August
Cultivation (control of weeds)	April to October
Control of rose troubles	May to mid—October
Summer pruning	mid—June to mid—September
Removal of rootstock shoots	April to October

ROSES IN LANDSCAPING

A rose has many advantages over other shrubs. It blooms for long periods and the effect and range of colour of the flowers is remarkable. The autumn colouring of the foliage, the shape and colour of the hips, sometimes supplemented by decorative thorns, makes the rose a must in landscape schemes of all kinds. In large parks, housing developments, city green belts and exhibition grounds as well as alongside modern highways the rose has a special place in formal beds. In order to enhance the natural beauty of the rose the grower places it in a suitable setting. A background such as dark evergreens or some other type of hedging is often very effective as are a green, well-tended lawn or light-coloured walls.

The wide range of species and varieties allows each gardener to select roses suitable for his own particular garden scheme, the required effect being produced by isolated groups as well as continuous beds. In order to make the best use of the various types of roses it is necessary to bear in mind the most important characteristics of different groups.

Multi-flowered roses — polyanthas, hybrid polyanthas, floribundas and large-flowered floribundas — bear rich clusters of what are sometimes entirely simple flowers, usually without any fragrance. The beauty of this type lies in the abundance of blooms and length of the flowering season, and is therefore best suited for mass planting. From the aesthetic point of view it will also be important to see that the colours of the individual varieties harmonize with one another as well as with the background against which they are grown, whether tree, shrub, water or wall. An example of such an arrangement could be, for example, a solitary group of 'Orange Sensation' placed in front of a typically irregular backdrop of juniper, say *Juniperus squamata* 'Meyeri'. Large-flowered floribundas, besides being massed in irregularly or geometrically shaped beds in large landscape schemes, are also excellent as an almost perpetually blooming hedge in small gardens. In large schemes 'Queen Elizabeth' is one variety that will satisfy even the most discriminating of rose lovers if planted in solitary groups of three to five sufficiently far from a backdrop of dark green yew trees (*Taxus baccata*). If a flower bed is planted entirely with one variety of flori-bunda, it makes it possible to have the bed fully covered. In sunken rose gardens if the height and habit of growth of the individual varieties have been correctly estimated, they can be planted in large geometrical patterns resembling a painter's palette laid out in the grass.

Hybrid tea roses are primarily valued for the individual beauty of the blooms and, in many instances, also for their

Roses in combination with other shrubs and trees for the patio garden
1 — *Pinus nigra (P. austriaca)*, 2 — 'Super Star', 'Peace', 'Queen of Bermuda', 3 — 'Lilli Marlene', 'Orange Sensation', 'Allgold', 4 — 'Queen Elizabeth', 5 — *Pyracantha coccinea* 'Kasan', 6 — 'Heidelberg', 'New Dawn', 'Paul's Scarlet Climber', 7 — *Rosa* x *highdownensis*, 8 — *Rosa roulettii*, 'Baby Masquerade', 'Yellow Doll', 9 — 'The Fairy', 10 — *Rosa* x *hugoptera*, 11 — *Magnolia soulangiana*, 12 — *Tilia parviflora*, 13 — *Larix decidua (L. europaea)*, 14 — *Taxus baccata*, 15 — *Juniperus squamata* 'Meyeri', 16 — *Cotoneaster praecox*

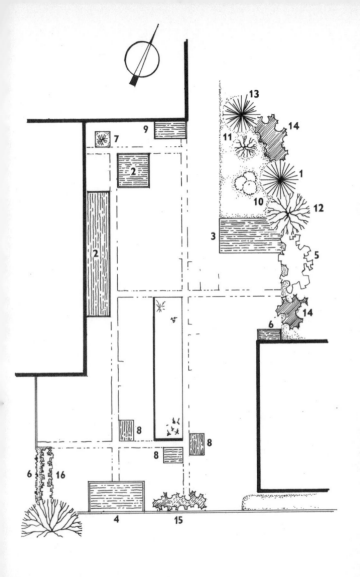

fragrance, so when planting these roses they should be placed so that their attractive features can be admired at close hand.

In addition to the colour and type of flower the shape of roses is of primary importance in landscaping. Shape is determined by three features: the type of rose, its branching and flowering habits; the way in which it is grafted on to a stock; and the manner of its training. A short summary of the most popular shapes and how they have come about will perhaps be a guide in selection.

1. Bush roses branch from the ground and this is the normal habit of hybrid tea, floribunda, shrub and miniature roses. These roses are budded on to the stock at ground level, and by pruning kept into tidy shapes. Miniature bush, dwarf bush and bush roses give a wide range of size and usage either for the front of the border or for formal beds.

2. Standard roses are hybrid teas and floribundas grafted on to strong briar stems which form a bare trunk with a head of branches on the top like a small tree. Half and full-standards differ in the height of the 'trunk'. Weeping standards are produced by grafting ramblers or climbing roses on to briar stems. The hanging branches are often trained over a frame so that the total appearance is that of a weeping tree.

3. Pillar roses are vigorous climbers or ramblers trained up stakes or old trees to form an erect and elegant-looking tree useful as a background for hardy perennials or for formal beds of bush roses.

ROSES AND PERENNIALS

Planting roses in combination with perennials would have provoked vociferous objections on the part of rose lovers only a few years ago. However, there is ample evidence that if selected with a sensitive eye the flowers of perennials not only fill in the period before roses are in flower but can also form interesting colour compositions with the rose blooms in the summer months. This is especially so in small gardens which cannot devote large areas to one genus.

When planted together with roses perennials are grown in small independent groups or clumps located at a suitable distance from the roses so as not to impede the easy performance of all cultivating operations necessary for maintaining them in good condition. Crocuses, small species tulips, narcissi and other bulbous plants are excellent during spring. After the flowering period their foliage, before dying away, forms a neutral cover which in no way disturbs the colour effect of the rose blooms. During the summer months the contrast of the delicate pink or yellow of the roses and the azure or dark blue of the long sprays of delphiniums is lovely. Not so well suited is the combination of red roses and lilies *(Lilium regale)*, not so much because of the colour as because of the shape and arrangement of the lilies. Towards autumn the somewhat poorer quality of the foliage at the base of the bush of certain large-flowered varieties can be concealed by low-growing asters or Michaelmas daisies.

ROSES AND TREES

The effect of roses of suitably selected varieties planted in formal or informal beds in the garden can be enhanced by the presence of trees. Excellent in the small garden are, for example, the creeping juniper tree *Juniperus sabina tamariscifolia*, the unsymmetric juniper *Taxus cuspidata*, and the fan-like *Chamaecyparis obtusa 'Nana gracilis'*. Of the deciduous trees and shrubs best suited are species such as *Ceanothus americanus*, *Cotoneaster horizontalis saxatilis*, *Evonymus fortunei* 'Vegetus', *Lonicera alpigena* and *Corylopsis pauciflora*. The selection of trees depends on the type and variety of the rose plants. Only dwarf trees can be considered for the miniature varieties and in addition the entire layout must be very precise. Also very effective in large schemes is the combination of the tall *Rosa hugonis*, for instance, placed in the lawn some 10—15 m (30—45 ft) in front of a group of mature firs.

In patio and courtyard gardens, dwarf roses in borders around miniature pools, benches and walls make a very effective combination with prostrate carpeting perennials, rock garden plants and dwarf Japanese maples or decorative grasses. A light-coloured wall in the background of such a layout is brightened most effectively by red climbing roses.

Shrub roses with their loose and, in many instances, vigorous growth are best planted in larger landscape schemes. The character of the given species and varieties must be kept in mind when deciding whether to plant them independently or in a continuous border. In either case these roses are shown to best advantage when planted against a backdrop of bushes, tall trees or buildings. Best suited for continuous plantings are certain true species such as *Rosa alba*, *R. cinnamomea*, *R. eglanteria*, *R. filipes*, *R. foetida*, *R. moyesii*, *R. multiflora*, *R. rubrifolia*, *R. rugosa*, *R. setipoda*. Good as solitaries are 'Frühlingsduft', 'Maigold', *R. hugonis*, and *Rosa* x *hugoptera*.

Climbing roses, unlike bedding roses (floribunda and hybrid tea varieties), are also excellent for growing on specially prepared supports such as pergolas or for growing up among the branches of old trees. They can also be used for cascading down rough banks and for rambling over old tree stumps. Ideal for this purpose is the unpretentious *Rosa* x *paulii*. Some varieties that are not too vine-like, for example 'New Dawn' and 'Paul's Scarlet Climber', are excellent as freely growing solitaries in the lawn against a backdrop of trees or bushes, but need careful training.

In planting roses together with trees it is necessary to keep in mind not only the aesthetic aspect but also to observe the important demands of both for their normal and undisturbed development. Where roses are planted in front of taller bushes and trees their distance from these increases in proportion with their height. Besides cutting off the light these tall neighbours would also rob the roses of vital nutrients and moisture.

ROSES AND ROCK GARDEN PLANTS

The use of roses in rock gardens was first made possible by the increase in the range of miniature roses, but it is still not a very common practice. The gardener must know a great deal about the characteristics of rock garden plants and roses and must also have a great measure of good taste to grow the two types in a combination that will be effective. Of the miniature roses good ones for this purpose are 'Happy', 'Perla de Alcanada', 'Yellow Doll', 'Baby Masquerade' and 'The Fairy'. Rock garden plants that easily become rampant should never be planted next to roses grown in clumps.

GROWING ROSES IN CONTAINERS

Many city dwellers have no garden, yet they, too, would like to grow roses. Few roses are suitable for growth as house plants, mainly because of the amount of room required by their root systems. The rose is a deep-rooting plant and if the growth of its roots is limited by the space of a flowerpot then the top of the plant is also unable to develop as it should. Attempts have been made to overcome this problem by using specially prepared nutritive solutions, but plants rarely survive for long. However, better results can be obtained by growing roses in troughs or tubs on a balcony. One thing that should be kept in mind, however, is that the plants must not be exposed to strong winds or scorching sun on hot summer days. The planting and pruning of roses grown in containers is the same as in ordinary cultivation in the open. The earth in the container should be good top soil with added composted soil and well-rotted farmyard manure. Best results, however, are obtained by regular use of a compound fertilizer especially for roses. It is most important to ensure that there are drainage holes in the container used so that water will not swamp the roots and cause them to rot. Broken crock is used at the base to prevent soil from being washed out. Wise watering is essential. Almost any type of rose may be grown in a tub or trough. Strong-growing hybrid teas such as 'Peace', 'Super Star', 'Gail Border' or climbers such as 'Mermaid' and 'Maigold' are recommended.

THE IMPORTANCE OF ROSES

In the previous chapters, the role of the rose in the history of mankind has been very briefly discussed in accordance with the extent of this book. Today the growing of roses has become an important activity that is the concern of numerous nurserymen and horticultural institutions all over the world.

Attar of roses is an important ingredient in some cosmetic preparations. Today it is produced chiefly in Bulgaria. The yield is very small: 500 kg (about 1,102 lb) of rose petals, which is about 3,000,000 blooms, are required for 1 kg (roughly 2 lb) of attar of roses. Roses are also of importance for the food and pharmaceutical industries, which prize the fleshy hips above all for their high vitamin C content.

In some countries roses comprise up to thirty per cent of the total production of ornamental trees and shrubs grown in nurseries, and for years roses have been among the most widely cultivated blooms for the cut-flower trade.

The need for roses, like the need for flowers as such, may in its way serve as an indication of the living standard; and therefore we can but hope that the popularity of roses will continue to grow and that it will do so in all countries of the world.

PLATES

KEY TO THE PLATE DESCRIPTIONS

The species and cultivars are divided into groups according to the garden classification.

The name is followed by the origin of the species or the name of the grower, year of introduction and the name of the parent plants.

ABBREVIATIONS

Min.	— *miniature*	Cl.	— *climber*
Pol.	— *polyantha*	Ramb.	— *rambler*
F.	— *floribunda*	S.	— *shrub*
H.T.	— *hybrid tea*	R.	— *rootstock*

'BABY MASQUERADE'　　　　　Min.

MATH. TANTAU, 1955; 'Tom Thumb' x 'Masquerade'

This plant has a compact growth reminiscent of the floribunda 'Masquerade', one of the two parent plants. It attains
a height of about 30—45 cm (1—1½ ft), is healthy and very
free-flowering. The flower is double, yellow edged with pink,
without fragrance.

Lovers of bright-coloured roses plant 'Baby Masquerade'
in rock gardens and miniature beds or else grow it in pots or
in the front of the border.

This variety is sometimes known as 'Baby Carnival'.

'CORALIN' Min.

P. DOT, 1955; 'Mephisto' x 'Perla de Alcanada'

This dense, upright plant grows to a height of 30 cm (1 ft). The young stems are reddish at first, turning green with age. The foliage is a glossy green. The flowers, measuring up to 4 cm (1½ in) across, are double (forty petals), coral red, without fragrance. This variety bears as many as ten flowers at a time but — unlike 'Baby Masquerade', for example — they are individual blooms borne on separate stems and do not form clusters.

'Coralin' is a very vigorous and healthy variety which, if well cared for, will bloom continuously throughout the whole season. Severe frosts will not kill it even in winters without snow, especially if it is grafted on *R. rubiginosa* stock. It is most effective if planted in small groups in the rock garden.

ROSA CHINENSIS MINIMA   Min.

True species, known in Europe since 1815

This is an erect plant with compact, freely branching green stems and only occasional thorns. It attains a maximum height of 30 cm (1 ft). The leaves, about 5 cm (2 in) long, comprise five to seven elongate, sharp-toothed leaflets a maximum of 2 cm ($\frac{3}{4}$ in) across and coloured pink.

R. chinensis minima, or 'Fairy Rose' as it is called in English, is grown in pots or troughs. If well cared for it can be an attractive addition to the rock garden when planted in clumps among suitable dwarf shrubs. The leaves are slightly prone to black spot.

This rose has at different times been classified under the following names:

R. roulettii CORREVON; *R. semperflorens minima* SIMS; *R. laurentiae* TRATTINICK; *R. lawrenceana* SWEET; *R. indica pumila* THORY.

'ROSINA' Min.

P. DOT, 1942; 'Eduardo Toda' x *Rosa roulettii*

This plant has a dense growth and reaches a height of up to 45 cm (1½ ft). It is remarkably healthy and bears an abundance of flowers. The foliage is a dark glossy green. The semi-double flowers (with an average of sixteen petals) are borne singly, or more usually in clusters, are well formed and without fragrance. The colour is a bright golden-yellow which remains practically unchanged by the effects of the weather. The fully opened flower measures up to 4 cm (1½ in) across.

'Rosina' is an older but nevertheless continually popular variety suitable for the rock garden or smaller beds in the company of dwarf or compact growing perennials.

This rose is sometimes known as 'Josephine Wheatcroft' or 'Yellow Sweetheart'.

'THE FAIRY'

Pol.

J. A. BENTALL, 1932; dwarf sport from 'Lady Godiva'

This rose has a spreading growth with stems attaining a length of 40 cm (1¼ ft); it is short and bushy. The leaves are small, pale green and very glossy. The double flowers, growing in small thick clusters, are whitish to pale pink in summer, intense pink in autumn; full-blown blooms are always paler than the buds. The flower is without fragrance.

Its healthy growth and practically continuous flowering make this variety an excellent rose for the rock garden. It is not suited for cultivation in pots because the reduction of sunlight in the late autumn causes poor growth and flowers that are a dirty white with almost no trace of pink.

This rose is sometimes known as 'Sweet Pink'.

'YELLOW DOLL'   Min.

R. S. MOORE, 1962; 'Golden Glow' x 'Zee'

This plant has a slow but erect growth, forming fairly strong stems terminating as a rule in a single flower. The pointed bud is a rich yellow, the flower pale yellow, high-centred, double, about 2.5 cm (1 in) across, and abundant but without fragrance. The leaves usually comprise five narrow pointed leaflets with fine sharp serrations.

'Yellow Doll' is currently the best of the miniature yellow varieties. It is well suited for growing in the rock garden and in containers.

'POUR TOI' Min.

P. DOT, 1946; 'Eduardo Toda' x 'Pompon de Paris'

This plant has a compact bushy growth and is only 20 cm (8 in) high. The stems are slender, almost filament-like, bearing a very small semi-double flower (fifteen petals at the most). The flower is white with a slightly yellow centre and without fragrance.

'Pour Toi' is a good variety for growing in a clay-peat soil in a pot.

This rose is sometimes known as 'Para Ti' or 'Wendy'.

'ALAIN'

F. MEILLAND, 1946; ('Guinée' x 'Skyrocket') x 'Orange Triumph'

This plant is of a spreading habit and attains a medium height. The leaves are dark green, glossy, medium-sized. The bright carmine-red double flowers grow in medium-sized clusters and are slightly fragrant, characterized by ovoid buds.

'Alain' is a very popular rose for its healthy growth and rich florescence. Large plantings should be placed against a light background to avoid the sombre effect the masses of dark blooms would otherwise produce.

'CAROL AMLING' F.

C. M. AMLING and BERTRAM, 1953; sport from 'Garnette'

This rose has an upright, compact growth. The individual stems branch easily, are firm yet flexible and terminate in several blooms. The flower is double, low-centred, slightly fragrant and coloured a delicate silvery-pink. Cut flowers will last twelve or more days in the vase. The foliage is reddish at first, later turning a glossy dark green.

'Carol Amling' is currently one of the most popular and most widely cultivated floribundas for the cut-flower trade. It is the most floriferous of the sports from 'Garnette'. In garden terminology, however, the term 'garnette' is used for other varieties as well, such as 'Zorina', even though this is not a sport from 'Garnette', being distinguished only by a marked resemblance of habit.

This rose is occasionally known as 'Carol'.

'CONCERTO'

F. MEILLAND, 1953; 'Alain' x 'Floradora'

This rose has a fairly free vigorous growth, reaching a medium height. The stems are covered with abundant glossy dark green foliage. The flowers have twelve to seventeen orange-red petals and a slight fragrance, and although rather small are very freely produced.

'Concerto', like 'Alain', is very good for planting in large beds.

'MASQUERADE' F.

E. S. BOERNER, 1949; 'Goldilocks' x 'Holiday'

This vigorous, and on the whole very healthy, rose reaches a taller than average height. The stems are erect, but later slightly bent under the weight of the large clusters of flowers. The foliage is a semi-glossy dark green, unusually free from disease. The flowers are yellow, pink and crimson. This variety of colours was the decisive factor in determining the rose's name — 'Masquerade'.

The ever-healthy foliage and the great vitality of this variety are a guarantee that with normal care the plant will bloom from early summer until the onset of the first autumn frosts. Its healthy growth would seem to make this an ideal rose for the largest beds; however, this has not proved to be so because of the excessive brightness of the flowers, which many rose lovers consider a drawback.

'PAPRIKA'

MATH. TANTAU, 1958; 'Märchenland' x 'Red Favourite'

This medium tall plant has a vigorous growth. The stems become slightly spreading with age. The glossy olive-green foliage is an excellent foil for the bright brick-red flowers. The colour of the blooms is reminiscent of a ripe red paprika and hence the name; it also won this rose awards at several international shows. In damp summers it is liable to black spot and it is necessary to spray mass plantings with the required solution as a preventive measure.

'GOLDEN SLIPPERS'

GORDON J. VON ABRAMS, 1961;
'Goldilocks' x un-named seedling

F.

This is a low-growing, moderately vigorous plant of slightly spreading habit with abundant foliage. The leaves are oval and a glossy olive-green. The flowers are semi-double with eighteen to twenty-five petals, their colour changing as they open from golden-yellow at first to yellow on the outside and yellow mingled with red on the inside when in full bloom.

The delicate colouring of its flowers recommends 'Golden Slippers' for smaller plantings in combination with other varieties such as 'Lilli Marlene' and 'Rimosa'.

'YELLOW PINOCCHIO' F.

E. S. BOERNER, 1949; 'Goldilocks' x 'Marionette'

This is a plant of upright habit which reaches a medium height. The stems branch freely and are terminated by dense clusters of flowers. The double blooms (forty-five petals) are large and fragrant. The colour is a creamy apricot-yellow. In damp summers it tends to bloom poorly. The foliage is a dark glossy green.

'Yellow Pinocchio' is a bedding rose effective in combination with 'Masquerade' as it somewhat softens the excessive brightness of the latter's blooms.

'ELIZABETH OF GLAMIS' F.

SAM McGREDY, 1963; 'Spartan' x 'Highlight'

This rose is compact, vigorous and floriferous and of medium growth. Pruning is no setback as it quickly sets new buds. The foliage is a glossy pale green. The buds are pointed, 3—4 cm (1¼—1½ in) long. The large semi-double flowers, up to seven on one stem, are a soft salmon colour, richer in the heart and with a delicate golden tinge.

'Elizabeth of Glamis' is recommended for smaller groups.

'JAN SPEK'

F.

SAM McGREDY, 1966; 'Clare Grammerstorf' x 'Faust'

This is a vigorous and slightly spreading plant of short bushy growth clothed with attractive dense dark green foliage. The flowers open successively to form abundant clusters. The buds are shallow rounded cones with reddish-brown petals on the outside. The low-centred, double, open flowers are a rich glowing yellow and slightly fragrant.

This excellent floribunda bears the name of its breeder, who also produced the hybrid tea 'Spek's Yellow', very popular at one time. 'Jan Spek' is recommended primarily as a bedding rose for it sheds its petals after they have faded and therefore does not require a great deal of attention.

'AMERICA'S JUNIOR MISS'   F.

E. S. BOERNER, 1964; 'Seventeen' x 'Demure' seedling

This is a vigorous, upright plant with many flower-bearing stems. The olive-green leaves are medium-sized. The flowers are high-centred, a delicate coral-pink and slightly fragrant.

In recent years 'America's Junior Miss' has become a very popular variety for glasshouse cultivation for the quantity and quality of its blooms are almost on a par with those of sports from 'Garnette'. When grown outdoors the flowers are not of as high a quality, but those who like this colour will be well satisfied with the plant's healthy growth and abundance of flowers.

'LILLI MARLENE' F.

R. KORDES, 1959; ('Our Princess' x 'Rudolf Timm') x 'Ama'

This is a vigorous, bushy rose of medium growth. The stems branch well and terminate in big trusses of largish semi-double flowers of a velvety fiery-red, without fragrance. The foliage is dark green and healthy.

'Lilli Marlene' is an outstanding variety with very hardy flowers, well suited for even the largest beds. As with 'Alain', the dark red of its flowers requires careful selection of its site in landscaping schemes.

'MILENA'   F.

L. VEČEŘA, 1964; bud sport from 'Queen Elizabeth'

This rose has a vigorous growth and is tall-growing. The stems are strong and flexible, coloured red when budding. The leaves are a dark glossy green with red veining. The flowers grow singly on long stems; if exceptionally vigorous there may be three to seven to a stem. They are double and coloured a deep carmine-pink. The bud is shapely and elongate.

'Milena' is an induced mutation produced by the irradiation of seeds from 'Queen Elizabeth'. It differs from the original variety mainly in the deeper pink colour of its flowers. It is well suited for large landscape schemes where its height is not a handicap, or in small solitary groups against a background of medium-sized conifers. In small gardens it is excellent as an untrimmed, almost continuously flowering hedge.

'INDEPENDENCE' F.

R. KORDES, 1950; 'Baby Château' x 'Crimson Glory' F₂ seedling

---

'Independence' is the name given this rose by the English-speaking world in preference to 'Sondermeldung' meaning 'special bulletin'. Even though this was a 'special bulletin' put out by Kordes — and a very pleasant one for rose-growers — nevertheless for postwar Europe it was too reminiscent of the special military bulletins of the war years.

The shrub has a strong, medium growth of spreading habit. The individual stems terminate in one or more short, seemingly truncated buds. The scentless flower is large, double and well formed, of an intense orange-scarlet at first and later geranium-red, blueing in the final stages. The outside of the petals is shaded black at the base. The foliage is a glossy dark green.

In its day 'Independence' was a very valuable addition to the assortment of existing varieties chiefly for its unusual and previously unknown geranium-red colouring. In recent years great susceptibility to black spot has caused a decline in its popularity among growers. It is healthiest grown as a standard, a form in which its slightly pendent habit is very effective.

'NORDIA'   F.

NIELS POULSEN, 1967

This is an erect and very vigorous plant of medium height. Marked by great vitality, it has a growth period extending until late in the autumn. The flowers, one to five to a stem, are double and a glowing orange-red that is very effective. The finely serrated leaves are a glossy dark green and remarkably healthy.

'Nordia' is an excellent addition to the assortment of all-purpose roses. It is a good bedding rose and also good for cutting.

'ORANGE SENSATION'

F.

G. DE RUITER, 1961

This is an upright and healthy plant of medium height. The branching, rather compact growth produces clusters of five to seven flowers. These are double (twenty-four petals) and a brilliant salmon-pink. The dark green foliage is plentiful.

'Orange Sensation' is a free-flowering and healthy variety with a pleasant fragrance. The unusual colour of the blooms changes only slightly as they fade. These characteristics rank this rose among the current top bedding varieties, suitable even for the largest beds; its use in the garden is unlimited.

'ORANGE SPECIAL' F.

G. DE RUITER, 1957; sport from 'Salmon Perfection'

This is a low-growing, upright variety with comparatively little foliage. The leaves are small and are matt green. The stems bear large clusters of flowers, as many as twenty to a cluster. The buds are short, partially open and as if truncated. Even the largest of the double flowers is no more than 3 cm ($1\frac{1}{4}$ in) across, with orange-scarlet petals which withstand the effects of the weather very well. The broad clusters of rather small blooms completely fill the space of the bed at the height of the flowering season.

'Orange Special' is one of the best of the small-flowering floribundas and has many uses.

'RIMOSA'   F.

F. MEILLAND, 1958; 'Goldilocks' x 'Perla de Montserrat'

This plant is of medium height and of a dense, branching growth which produces many smaller clusters, each containing several semi-double flowers (eighteen to twenty-five petals). The colour is a rich lemon-yellow at first, later becoming pale lemon-yellow.

'Rimosa' is a variety with foliage that is almost completely disease-resistant and blooms that fall easily when faded. One disadvantage of this rose, however, is that the petals soon turn white in hot sunny weather. Despite this 'Rimosa' is a good variety, even for larger beds.

'RUDOLPH TIMM'   F.

R. KORDES, 1951; ('Johannes Böttner' x 'Magnifica') x ('Baby Château' x 'Else Poulsen')

This is a vigorous, upright plant of medium height. The stems bear large flat clusters of semi-double blooms. The open flowers are 5 cm (2 in) across on the average, fragrant, white shading to red at the edges. They resemble petunias when fully opened. The foliage is a glossy pale green.

'Rudolph Timm' is especially suitable for large beds as the large clusters of flowers amply fill their space.

'RUMBA'

S. POULSEN, 1958; 'Masquerade' x ('Poulsen's Bedder' x 'Floradora')

This plant has a broad spreading growth of medium height. The stems are a rich green with a dark reddish-brown tinge. The foliage is a glossy dark green und unusually free from disease. The flowers are carried in large trusses and are of reddish-pink changing during growth to golden-yellow edged with red in the fully opened bloom.

'Rumba', together with the varieties 'Charleston' and 'Samba', belongs to the 'dance' group and is the healthiest of them all. 'Samba', however, is far more striking in the first stage of bloom. 'Rumba' is seen to best advantage when planted in smaller more intimate settings where the beauty and diversity of colour of its flowers can be easily admired.

'ICEBERG'

R. KORDES, 1956; 'Robin Hood' x 'Virgo'

This strong-growing plant is taller than average with a slender rather loose growth. The stems are long and slightly runner-like with much glossy pale green foliage. The flowers are carried in large trusses, medium-sized, open, double, slightly fragrant. The colour is pure white when fully open but tinted with pink in the bud.

'Iceberg' is best suited either for planting in beds behind smaller coloured varieties or in small solitary groups. It is not recommended for large beds as the shrubs are not bushy enough and the flowers do not fill out the space to a sufficient degree.

This rose is also known as 'Schneewittchen' and 'Fée des Neiges'.

'QUEEN ELIZABETH'   F.

W. LAMMERTS, 1954; 'Charlotte Armstrong' x 'Floradora'

This is a very vigorous tall-growing plant of upright habit and almost thornless wood. The flowers are produced on long flexible stems both singly and in small trusses of three to seven blooms. The buds are long and slender. The double flowers (thirty-five petals on average) are a clear carmine-pink with a delicate fragrance. The leaves are large, dark green and semi-glossy.

The large-flowered floribunda 'Queen Elizabeth' is exceptionally healthy. It is excellent in large beds as well as in solitary groups.

'ZAMBRA'

F.

M. L. MEILLAND, 1961; ('Goldilocks' x 'Fashion') x
('Goldilocks' x 'Fashion')

This rose is moderately vigorous, tall-growing and not too
bushy. The foliage is a semi-glossy pale green. The flowers
have only ten to fifteen petals and are slightly fragrant. The
colour is unique among roses, a rich flame-orange with a
golden reverse changing during growth to pale orange.

'Zambra' is good for smaller beds in the garden chiefly
because of the unusual colour of its blooms.

'ZORINA'   F.

E. S. BOERNER, 1963; 'Pinocchio' seedling x 'Spartan'

The vigorous, bushy growth of this variety is reminiscent of 'Garnette'. The stems are of medium height and well branched. The leaves with their coarse serrations are comparatively large in relation to the plant's habit. The double high-centred flowers, measuring 6 cm ($2\frac{1}{4}$ in) across, are carried in clusters. The colour is a brilliant salmon-pink fading only slightly in the sun throughout the entire flowering season.

'Zorina' is currently highly prized chiefly for its good crop of flowers in glasshouse cultivation for the cut-flower trade. It also grows and flowers well when planted outdoors, but it is necessary to cut off the faded blooms at regular intervals as the dead petals do not drop.

'ANVIL SPARKS' H. T.

E. F. H. MEYER, 1961

This is a healthy variety valued chiefly for its interesting flowers. The bud is elongate and well formed, while the flower is double with thirty to thirty-five petals and a very pleasant, intense fragrance..The colour is a fiery-red streaked with yellow, reminiscent of sparks flying from an anvil — hence its name 'Anvil Sparks'.

'Anvil Sparks' is a rose for those who like the unusual, even though the remarkable colouring is accompanied by other excellent features, namely the fragrance and the classic form of the flower.

This rose is also known as 'Ambossfunken'.

'ARLENE FRANCIS'   H. T.

E. S. BOERNER, 1957; 'Eclipse' seedling x 'Golden Scepter'

This plant is of medium height and has an abundance of glossy dark green foliage. The elongate pointed buds are 4—5 cm (1½—2 in) long and borne either singly or up to three to a stem. The flower is golden-yellow, 12 cm (4¾ in) across, and has a very marked fragrance. It withstands the effects of the weather well.

'BETTINA' H. T.

F. MEILLAND, 1953; 'Peace' x ('Mme Joseph Perraud' x 'Demain')

This is a vigorous, spreading plant of medium height. The stems are reddish in the fleshy stage, later brownish-green with small thorns. The leaves are medium-sized with a marked metallic sheen. The bud is bluntly conical, the ratio of the width to length being 3.5:5 cm (1¼:2 in). The double flower measures 9 cm (3½ in) across and has an average of forty-one orange to bronze-pink petals. It is slightly fragrant.

'Bettina' is a very popular variety suited for both outdoor and glasshouse cultivation. Cut flowers will last seven days in water.

'Dr A. J. VERHAGE'   H. T.

G. VERBEEK, 1960; 'Tawny Gold' x ('Baccara' x seedling)

This is a low-growing rose of upright habit. The strong, straight stems bear only one flower as a rule. The shape of the bud differs from that of most varieties; at about a third of its length the broad base suddenly becomes pointed giving the impression of an angular form. The ratio of width to length is 4.5 : 6.5 cm ($1\frac{3}{4}$: $2\frac{1}{2}$ in). The semi-double flower, with twenty to twenty-five petals, measures up to 16 cm ($6\frac{1}{4}$ in) across and has a very pleasant fragrance. It is golden-yellow, shaded with apricot.

The Dutch grower G. Verbeek succeeded in creating a masterpiece with this rose. It is a good forcing variety but it needs a warm position and good weather in the open garden. The flowers are of top-grade quality.

'PEACE'   H. T.

F. MEILLAND, 1945; 'Joanna Hill' x ('Charles P. Kilham' x
R. foetida bicolor seedling) x ('Charles P. Kilham' x 'Margaret
McGredy')

This is a very vigorous, slightly spreading plant of tall
growth. The young budding stems are green, turning greenish-brown with age, and scattered with broad greenish-
brown thorns. The decorative leaves are large, broad, and of
a metallic dark green. The stems are firm and terminate in
several massive buds, the ratio of width to length being
3.5 : 4.5—5 cm ($1\frac{1}{4}$: $1\frac{3}{4}$—2 in). The flower is exceptionally
large and full, with an average of fifty-two petals of a delicate
yellow with a shading of pink on the outer edges. In the
autumn blooms the delicate pink predominates over the
basic yellow colour. The flowers have a slight fragrance.

This rose is an outstanding and very popular variety, excellent both in solitary groups and massed in beds.

'Peace' is synonymous with 'Gioia', 'Gloria Dei' and
'Mme A. Meilland'.

'CHRYSLER IMPERIAL' H. T.

W. E. LAMMERTS, 1952; 'Charlotte Armstrong' x 'Mirandy'

This plant is moderately vigorous and of erect habit and medium height. The large leaves are dark green with markedly pale veining. Young shoots are red, mature stems brownish-green and firm, bearing two buds as a rule. The bud is short and conical, the ratio of width to length being 5 : 6.5 cm (2 : 2½ in). The double flower, measuring 12 cm (4¾ in) across, has fifty, velvety, dark carmine-red petals and a very rich perfume.

'Chrysler Imperial' is a variety with a growth period lasting well into the autumn. It is best suited for warmer locations where the late autumn blooms can develop well. The excellent foliage makes it possible to use this rose in isolated groups as a feature plant.

'JOHN S. ARMSTRONG' H. T.

H. C. SWIM, 1961; 'Charlotte Armstrong' x seedling

This vigorous, tall-growing, bushy rose is distinguished by blood-red stems during the budding period and very dark semi-glossy foliage. The buds are ovate, as if truncated at the top. The flowers are double, with forty petals, and measure 12 cm ($4\frac{3}{4}$ in) across. One stem may bear as many as nine dark velvety red blooms.

'John S. Armstrong' is an excellent, trouble-free variety which withstands rain well.

'KING'S RANSOM'   H. T.

D. MOREY, 1961; 'Golden Masterpiece' x 'Lydia'

This very robust and healthy plant is of medium height. The stems bear from one to five long ovate buds, 5—6 cm (2—2¼ in) in length, opening into large double flowers. The colour is a vivid golden-yellow which is altered very little by the effects of the weather. The foliage is a glossy pale green and greatly enhances the beauty of the plant.

'King's Ransom' is one of the best yellow roses for outdoor cultivation, but it is not at all suitable for glasshouse cultivation for the cut-flower trade. It is most effective when planted in small beds together with large-flowered red varieties or by itself against a background of darker-foliaged shrubs or conifers.

'ROYAL HIGHNESS' H. T.

H. C. SWIM and O. L. WEEKS, 1962; 'Virgo' x 'Peace'

This is a slender vigorous plant of healthy growth with matt dark green foliage. The flowers are double (forty to forty-five petals), high-centred, very fragrant and coloured a delicate, pale pink that is very beautiful. The buds are long and pointed.

'Royal Highness' bears its loveliest blooms at the beginning of the first flowering. It looks very effective when combined with 'Super Star' and 'Queen of Bermuda', for example.

'PIGALLE' H. T.

F. MEILLAND, 1951; 'Fantastique' x 'Boudoir' ('Paul Fromont')

This is a moderately vigorous rose of medium growth with abundant foliage. The flowers are 10 cm (4 in) across, very full and slightly fragrant. The petals (sixty) are comparatively small and coloured magenta to purple, with bluish shadings and a silvery-buff reverse.

Opinions vary as to the importance of this variety and its value. Perhaps the grower himself, F. Meilland, summed it up best when he wrote in his first description: 'You will admire and curse this rose at the same time'. This unique rose is principally a curiosity; for certain brief periods it surprises one with its unusual colouring, but under adverse weather conditions this is considered by some as unattractive.

'PERFECTA' H. T.

R. KORDES, 1957; 'Golden Scepter' x 'Karl Herbst'

This is a vigorous tall-growing plant with long strong stems and an upright habit. The young budding shoot is red, becoming greenish-brown with age, with sparse straight red thorns. The medium-large leaves are green with a delicate red sheen. The flower stem generally bears three to five blunt conical buds, the ratio of width to length being 4 : 6 cm ($1\frac{1}{2}$: $2\frac{1}{4}$ in). The open flower measures 15 cm (6 in) across and has thirty-five petals coloured creamy-white with a pink tinge shading to deep crimson at the edges. The fragrance is very strong and pleasant.

'Perfecta' and its sequel 'Kordes' Perfecta Superior', both have beautifully shaped, delicate flowers which, unfortunately, do not withstand wet weather well. Their cultivation in the open presents a number of problems in certain regions. The long stems and quality of the blooms make the rose suitable for the cut-flower trade.

This rose is synonymous with 'Kordes' Perfecta'.

'BLUE MOON' H. T.

MATH. TANTAU, 1964; un-named seedling x 'Sterling Silver'

This rose is of vigorous, upright, medium growth. The stems are green with abundant, semi-glossy, dark green foliage and with few thorns. Each stem bears one to five pointed ovate buds, 5—6 cm (2—2¼ in) long. The large, double flowers are well shaped and with a strong fragrance. The colour of the rose is violet changing to silvery-lilac when in full bloom.

'Blue Moon' belongs to the group of 'blue' roses; its main features, however, are the lovely form of the flower and spicy scent. It is good for cutting and much liked by flower arrangers.

This rose is synonymous with 'Mainzer Fastnacht' and 'Sissi'.

'VIRGO' H. T.

CH. MALLERIN, 1947; 'Pôle Nord' x 'Neige Parfum'

This plant is of vigorous, medium growth and upright habit. The stems are green, moderately prickly, with pale thin thorns. The foliage is a matt dark green. The flower stems usually bear only one bud; the ratio of width to length is 2.5 : 5 cm (1—2 in). The flower has twenty-four pure white petals, measures 12 cm (4¾ in) across and is slightly fragrant.

'Virgo' is a vigorous variety which looks effective in small beds combined with roses of other colours.

'PASCALI' H. T.

H. LENS, 1963; 'Queen Elizabeth' x 'White Butterfly'

The plant is of a vigorous, very upright habit and tall growth. The numerous stems, though fairly thin, are strong and flexible. The flowers (with twenty-three petals) are well formed and slightly fragrant. The dark green foliage is an excellent foil for the creamy-white blooms, which age to a pure white.

'Pascali' is an extremely good variety for small beds and as a decorative rose for cutting. It grows well in the open and cut flowers will last up to ten days.

'PICCADILLY' H. T.

SAM McGREDY, 1959; 'McGredy's Yellow' x 'Karl Herbst'

This vigorous, upright plant is of medium height. The many stems are covered with glossy dark green leaves slightly tinged with red. The large double flowers are bright red with a golden-yellow reverse, becoming pinker as the flower opens.

'Piccadilly' is a striking, very free-flowering variety suited both for large beds and for small gardens.

'PINK FAVOURITE'   H. T.

GORDON J. VON ABRAMS, 1956; 'Juno' x ('Georg Arends' x 'New Dawn')

This strong-growing plant makes an erect tall shrub. The large well-shaped flowers are carried on long upright stems with beautiful, very glossy pale green foliage. They are silvery-pink, double (twenty-five petals) and slightly fragrant. The buds are bluntly conical.

This variety is recommended for the garden for its reliability and resistance to disease.

'PINK PEACE'   H. T.

F. MEILLAND, 1959; ('Peace' x 'Monique') x ('Peace' x
'Mrs. John Laing')

This is a very vigorous tall-growing rose, upright and robust
in habit. The strong stems have few thorns and the abundant
foliage is a semi-glossy dark green. The flower stem usually
bears only one short conical bud; the ratio of width to length
is 4.5 : 6.5 cm (1¾ : 2½ in). The carmine-pink flower is
double, about 16 cm (6¼ in) across, with a pleasant fragrance.

'Pink Peace' is very like the variety 'Peace'. It is distinguished by leaves that are unusually free from disease. It is
most effective in small solitary groups or with other trees
or shrubs.

'BEAUTÉ' H. T.

CH. MALLERIN,1954; 'Mme Joseph Perraud'x un-named seedling

This is a medium-tall plant of erect habit. The young budding stems are green, changing to brown-green with age. The dark green foliage is semi-glossy. The unusually large buds — the ratio of width to length is 5 : 10 cm (2 : 4 in) — open into large flowers measuring up to 18 cm (7 in) across. The petals, twenty-four in number, are orange, those in the centre apricot-yellow. The bloom has a delicate fragrance.

The flower is of superb quality. The grower should devote particular care to preventive measures against black spot.

'RENDEZ-VOUS' H. T.

F. MEILLAND, 1953; 'Peace' x 'Europa'

This plant is of compact habit and of medium growth. The young stems are reddish but green when mature, thickly covered with thorns, and rather stiff. The large pale green leaves are leathery and semi-glossy. The flower stems terminate in a very fragile neck bearing a large elongate bud of a rich rose-pink; the ratio of width to length is 3.5 : 7 cm ($1\frac{1}{4}$: $2\frac{3}{4}$ in). The full-blown flower is double, bright pastel-pink and withstands the effects of the weather very well.

'Rendez-vous' is an excellent rose for cutting and will last ten days in water.

This rose is synonymous with 'Day of Triumph'.

'SUPER STAR'   H. T.

MATH. TANTAU, 1960; (seedling x 'Peace') x (seedling x
'Alpine Glow')

'Super Star', like 'Peace', was a landmark in rose-growing
circles, for it marked the beginning of a new era, the attainment of a completely new colour among roses. Add to this its
other outstanding qualities and there is no doubt that 'Super
Star' fully deserves its name.

A vigorous, tall-growing plant, it makes long well-
branched stems with matt dark green foliage. The young
shoots are reddish, becoming green with age and covered
with small pale brown thorns. Each stem bears only one
flower bud. Before it opens, however, some three to eight
side shoots grow out from the buds on the stem just below
the neck. When they are about 30—40 cm (1—1¼ ft) long
they bear flower buds that bloom shortly after the main
flower opens. To get single blooms on long stems it is necessary to cut off these side shoots as soon as they begin to show.

The flower bud is slender and conical, the ratio of width
to length being 3.5 : 7 cm (1¼ : 2¾ in). The well-formed,
double flower is 12 cm (5 in) across, with forty-two petals
of an almost fluorescent orange-red and a slight fragrance.
The colour remains practically constant and unchanged by
the effects of the weather.

'Super Star' can be used in many ways in all types of
garden and landscape schemes. It is a very healthy and free-
flowering variety.

It is sometimes known as 'Tropicana'.

'SUTTER'S GOLD'   H. T.

H.C. SWIM, 1950; 'Charlotte Armstrong' x 'Signora'

This plant is moderately vigorous, making tall, rather loose growth. The young shoot is pinkish, becoming brownish-green with age, and moderately prickly with large red-brown thorns. The large leaves are a glossy dark green. The stems are rather spindly, usually carrying just one flower bud. This is very slender, the ratio of width to length being 2.5 : 5 cm (1 : 2 in). The flower is double with thirty-two yellow petals strongly flushed with orange and deep pink with red-yellow veining on the reverse. It has a very strong fragrance.

'Sutter's Gold' can be used only in smaller landscape schemes, and is best of all in isolated groups. It is good for cutting.

'STERLING SILVER' H. T.

G. FISHER, 1957; seedling x 'Peace'

This rose is of moderate vigour and fairly scanty habit, making medium growth. The young budding shoots are lavender-pink, later green, and have few thorns. The foliage is a semi-glossy dark green. The stems generally bear only one upright bloom on a firm neck. The buds are broadly conical, the ratio of width to length being 3.5 : 4.5 cm ($1\frac{1}{4}$: $1\frac{3}{4}$ in). The open flower measures 11 cm ($4\frac{1}{4}$ in) across and has twenty-eight silvery-lilac petals and a very pleasant fragrance reminiscent of lemons.

As its name implies this variety is valued for its unusual silver or greyish-lilac colour, and for its marked fragrance. It should be planted only in the gardens of those who like such colours. The cut blooms last a long time in water.

'TAPESTRY'   H. T.

G. FISHER, 1958; 'Peace' x 'Mission Bells'

A moderately vigorous plant of loose habit, this rose is of medium growth. The foliage is very glossy and decorative and an excellent foil for the double (forty petals) flowers. The colour is a combination of light red, canary-yellow and pink. The fragrance is distinctive and pleasantly spicy.

'Tapestry' is a very striking variety, its prime attraction being the high-quality first blooms in early summer. It is most effective planted in combination with other hybrid teas.

'QUEEN OF BERMUDA'   F.

E. D. BOWIE, 1956; ('Independence' x 'Orange Triumph') x 'Bettina'

Erect and vigorous, this plant is very tall-growing and free-flowering. The young shoots are slightly reddish, but later change to dark green. The large dark green leaves are semi-glossy. There are one to five flowers to a stem; they measure 13 cm (5 in) across and have thirty-one bright scarlet petals with a distinctive black shading on the reverse. The size of the bud is 3 : 4.5 cm ($1\frac{1}{4}$: $1\frac{3}{4}$ in) in the ratio of width to length.

'Queen of Bermuda' is a very vigorous rose, good for isolated groups in landscape schemes and also a good decorative rose for cutting when grown in the open. In some countries it is used in glasshouse cultivation and has a rich harvest but the quality of the blooms does not equal that of a hothouse 'Baccara', which it greatly resembles both in colour and form and for which it is often mistaken.

'MEMORIAM'

H. T.

GORDON J. VON ABRAMS, 1961; ('Blanche Mallerin' x 'Peace')
x ('Peace' x 'Frau Karl Druschki')

This is a free-flowering plant of medium growth. The buds
are long and pointed. The flower has fifty to sixty petals and
is of immaculate form measuring 15 cm (6 in) across; it is
slightly fragrant. The colour is pastel-pink at first, changing
almost to white in the fully opened flower. The leaves are
a leathery dark green.

'Memoriam' can be used in the garden in small mixed
borders, but the flower, unfortunately, has comparatively
little resistance to wet weather.

'VIENNA CHARM' H. T.

R. KORDES, 1963; 'Golden Sun' x 'Chantré'

This is a vigorous upright plant of tall growth with strong firm shoots terminating, as a rule, in one flower bud. The shapely, high-centred flowers have twenty-seven petals and measure 15 cm (6 in) across. The colour is an unusual copper-orange, but the fragrance is slight. The leaves are large and dark green.

'Vienna Charm' is a remarkable rose valued primarily for the excellent quality of the blooms. It is best planted in small isolated groups. Its use is not widespread because of its low resistance to frost. It may need protection against black spot.

This rose is synonymous with 'Wiener Charme'.

'VEILCHENBLAU'

J. C. SCHMIDT, 1909; 'Crimson Rambler' x un-named seedling

This is a very vigorous plant growing to a height of 6 m (20 ft) when the stems are tied to a support. The leaves are large, pointed, glossy and a remarkably pale green. The small, semi-double flowers are about 3 cm ($1\frac{1}{4}$ in) across, and grow in large thick clusters. They come into flower in about the middle of June. The colour is violet at first, later fading to lilac with a white centre.

'Veilchenblau' is considered the first 'blue' rose. Today it is of historical interest only and is good for the collector's garden.

'FLAMMENTANZ'

R. KORDES, 1955; *R. eglanteria* hybrid x *R. kordesii*

This plant is distinguished by unusually vigorous growth, the strong stems measuring up to several metres in length. They are covered with large dark thorns. The foliage is leathery and dark green. The large scarlet flowers are arranged in thick clusters and are slightly fragrant. The first blooms open in about the middle of June.

'Flammentanz' is recommended for pergolas, high walls and pillars. In milder climates the adult plant can be trained to climb to a height of 6 m (20 ft) when tied to a support. It is also very effective when planted to cascade down banks.

'MRS. ARTHUR CURTISS JAMES' Cl.

W. D. BROWNELL, 1933; 'Mary Wallace' x seedling

Distinguished by vigorous growth, this plant makes long runner-like stems with glossy dark green leaves. The shapely elongate buds open successively from the middle of June. The large, double (twelve to twenty petals), glowing yellow flowers are open and fragrant.

Yellow climbing roses are not very numerous and that is why in this class the older varieties come into their own. The particular attraction of 'Mrs. Arthur Curtiss James' is the beauty of the flowers, seemingly scattered at random over the bush on older plants and blooming intermittently for practically the whole season.

This rose is also known as 'Golden Climber'.

'HEIDELBERG' Cl.

R. KORDES, 1959; 'Minna Kordes' x 'Floradora'

This is a vigorous healthy plant which grows to a height of 2—3 m (6½—10 ft) and is very free-flowering. The foliage is semi-glossy, leathery and a very good foil for the large high-centred flowers, which are 10 cm (4 in) across. These grow in thick clusters and bloom in the middle of June. The petals (thirty-two) are a glowing carmine-red, paler on the reverse, and withstand the vagaries of the weather very well.

'Heidelberg' can be used in many ways: as a free-growing bush, in a solitary group, trained to grow on a support and as a cut flower.

'NEW DAWN' Ramb.

H. A. DREER, 1930; sport from 'Dr W. Van Fleet'

A vigorous, spreading plant which can be trained to a height of 4 m (13 ft) when tied to a support. It is a very healthy grower. The good overall effect is heightened by the very glossy dark green foliage. The fragrant double flowers, borne in rich clusters, are a delicate flesh-pink. This is a perpetual-flowering variety that, except for a brief interval following the first bloom in the second half of June, bears flowers until autumn.

'New Dawn' is very widespread in its uses, being grown not only as a climber on supports but also as a free-growing shrub to ramble down banks and over unsightly objects in the garden such as old tree stumps.

'PAUL'S SCARLET CLIMBER'   Ramb.

W. PAUL, 1915; 'Paul's Carmine Pillar' x 'Soleil d'Or'

The vigorous, not too runner-like stems can be trained on a support to a height of 3—4 m (10—13 ft). The semi-double flowers are a bright scarlet-crimson, slightly fragrant, opening in the middle of June. The flowering is repeated but the first is more profuse.

'Paul's Scarlet Climber' is one of the hardiest and most widespread varieties. It can be used in several ways in the landscape scheme. It is very effective grown on a support against a light-coloured background; allowed to grow unrestrictedly it has a slightly pendent form and is very good for landscaping purposes. Grafted on to stems 2 m (6½ ft) tall of a species rootstock it grows into a small, wide-spreading tree with an umbrella-like crown that is very attractive when in flower.

ROSA x PAULII REHDER   Ramb.

G. PAUL, 1903; *R. arvensis x R. rugosa*

A very vigorous plant of sprawling habit, it can grow to
a height of 6 m (20 ft) if suitably trained. The strong shoots
are corky brown, covered with both large and small thorns;
their impenetrability is reminiscent of a Blackberry. The
dark foliage is very leathery and glossy. The buds are elongate with a slender point. The pure white single flowers are
up to 10 cm (4 in) across, and very free for about four to six
weeks beginning with the first half of June.

Rosa x *paulii* has not been sufficiently appreciated as a suitable shrub for landscape schemes to date. Its healthy growth,
trailing habit and beautiful, though single, blooms make it an
excellent cover for growing over banks and steep slopes as
well as for growing up through old trees or as an impene-
trable hedge on a simple support.

'MAIGOLD' S.

R. KORDES, 1953; 'Poulsen's Pink' x 'Frühlingstag'

The adult shrub has a spreading growth attaining a height of
3 m (10 ft) and a similar width. The shoots are robust, very
thorny and with abundant pale green foliage. The open,
semi-double flowers (fourteen petals) are bronze-yellow and
very fragrant. They bloom from about the last week of May
for four weeks — or even more if the weather is not too hot —
with a scattering of flowers later.

'Maigold' is an excellent rose for larger landscape schemes.
It is most effective as a pillar rose or a solitaire on the lawn.

ROSA WILLMOTTIAE HEMSLEY   S.

True species, native of western China, cultivated in Europe
since 1904

The adult shrub attains a height of 2.5 m (8 ft). It has long
shoots which branch little and are slightly pendent at the tip.
The greyish-green leaves are small and fern-like, resembling
down rather than foliage when viewed from a distance. When
in full flower, in July, the stems are covered with single
purplish-pink blooms measuring about 3 cm ($1\frac{1}{4}$ in) across.
Solitary groups at this time are very effective. Flowering is
not repeated.

The graceful foliage is very useful in flower decoration and
a good supply of young shoots for cutting can easily be produced by pruning, while at the same time keeping the rose
to manageable proportions.

R. willmottiae belongs to the subgroup Cinnamomeae.

'C. F. MEYER'

F. MÜLLER, 1899; *Rosa rugosa* hybrid x 'Gloire de Dijon'

A shrub of meagre, very upright habit it attains a height of 3 m (10 ft). The stems are robust and very thorny, terminating in double flowers with a very pleasant and concentrated fragrance. The flowers are pink at first, changing to silvery-pink when in full bloom. It bears flowers for about four weeks beginning in early June. The flowering is not repeated. In older plants the leathery foliage is present only at the ends of the stems.

'C. F . Meyer' is one of the most frost-resistant species, but its habit is not aesthetically striking. In landscape schemes it is most effective planted behind lower-growing roses with abundant foliage or together with other ornamental shrubs.

'DANSE DES SYLPHES'

CI.

CH. MALLERIN, 1959; 'Spectacular' x ('Peace' x 'Independence')

This plant is moderately vigorous with abundant foliage. When tied to a support the stems may grow to a height of 2.5 m (8 ft). The leaves are large and dark green. The large spherical clusters of flowers are coloured a rich geranium-red. Flowering is in the middle of June and will be repeated if the blooms are cut as soon as they fade.

'Danse des Sylphes' can be grown with or without a support. Free-growing plants make very nice solitary groups.

'FRÜHLINGSMORGEN'

R. KORDES, 1942; ('E. G. Hill' x 'Cathrine Kordes') x
R. spinosissima altaica

This moderately vigorous, slightly spreading shrub attains a height of 1.5 m (5 ft). The single, open blooms are a rich yellow, with cherry-pink shading towards the edges and a chestnut-brown anther and stamens which create a truly striking colour effect. Flowering begins in the first half of June and is not repeated; there are usually a few late flowers at the end of summer.

The distinctive beauty of the blooms assures 'Frühlingsmorgen' a place in the garden of every rose connoisseur.

'COCKTAIL'

F. MEILLAND, 1957; ('Independence' x 'Orange Triumph') x
'Phyllis Bide'

This shrub is not very large and grows to a height of only 1 m
(3 ft) in the most favourable climates. The pointed buds open
into single flowers, 5 cm (2 in) across, of geranium-red
shading to primrose-yellow in the centre. The glossy dark
green foliage is decorative.

'Cocktail' is a good rose for intensively tended landscape
schemes as a solitaire, for example, grown on a simple ladder
or low rail alongside steps.

'NEVADA'

P. DOT, 1927; 'La Giralda' x *R. moyesii* seedling

This is a vigorous shrub growing to a height of 2 m (6½ ft). The stems are very erect, arching slightly at the tip. The large, single flowers are delicate pink at first, creamy-white when in full bloom. Flowering is usually repeated towards the end of summer but is not as abundant as the spring bloom. The late summer flowers are pink with a carmine tinge. The blooms are without fragrance.

'Nevada' is a very good rose for solitary groups in larger landscape schemes.

ROSA DAVIDII CRÉPIN   S.

True species from western China, introduced to Europe in 1908

This rose has a very vigorous, somewhat spreading growth reaching a height of 3 m (10 ft) under favourable conditions. There are not many thorns but they are large and show up well. As a rule the leaves consist of nine dark green leaflets; they are semi-glossy, very leathery, and have coarse serrations. The flower stems bear three to seven buds and grow in trusses comprising twenty or more buds. The form of the bud is a rounded cone with very long sepals and an elongate, slightly pubescent ovary. The single flowers are pink, 5 cm (2 in) across at the most, and come into flower in June soon after *R. moyesii*. The hips are very slender and elongate, red when ripe and pendent. The flowers, and later the hips, on *R. davidii* are well spaced. When in flower the trusses resemble tufts of pink feathers.

This rose is most suitable for larger landscape schemes. It belongs to the subgroup Cinnamomeae.

ROSA FOETIDA BICOLOR S.

(JACQUIN) WILLMOTT

True species, grown in Europe since 1590

This shrub has a moderately vigorous loose growth, reaching a height of about 1.5 m (5 ft). The leaves, bearing seven to nine leaflets, are rounded and about 6 cm (2¼ in) long. The shoots are light chestnut-brown with thin light-coloured thorns here and there. The single flowers begin blooming during the last week in May, opening in succession; the flowering is not repeated. The petals are two-toned (hence the term *bicolor* in the name), of a rich yellow at the base shading to an intense coppery orange-red towards the edges with a yellow reverse. For sheer brilliance, there is nothing quite equal to it among roses.

Rosa foetida bicolor is known to gardeners as the Austrian Copper Rose. It has been grown in specimen groups in parks for centuries past and is also to be found in new and recent plantings.

It belongs to the subgroup Pimpinellifoliae and is also known under the following synonyms: *R. lutea punicea* (MILLER) R. KELLER; *R. punicea* MILLER; *R. bicolor* JACQUIN; *R. lutea bicolor* SIMS; *R. eglanteria punicea* THORY; *R. aurantiaca* VOSS.

ROSA GALLICA L.   S.

True species, grown in Europe since 1500

The adult shrub grows to a height of about $1\frac{1}{4}$ m (4 ft) and is of slightly arching habit. The stems have a few reddish thorns with a slight bloom. The leaves have five to seven leaflets, are rich green and about 10 cm (4 in) long. The single flowers up to 8 cm ($3\frac{1}{4}$ in) across are of a rich dark velvety red. They come into flower at the end of May. The light red hips are about 3 cm ($1\frac{1}{4}$ in) long and slightly prickly.

R. gallica is also known as the Gallic or French Rose. It is native to central southern Europe and western Asia. It is one of the wild roses that make side shoots from the base, and is probably one of the ancestors of garden roses in Europe.

It belongs to the subgroup Gallicanae and has the following synonyms: *R. austriaca* GRANTZ; *R. olympica* DONN; *R. rubra* LAMARCK; *R. sylvatica* GATERAU; *R. grandiflora* SALISBURY.

ROSA x HIGHDOWNENSIS HILLIER   S.

Probably a hybrid of *R. moyesii*, grown since 1928

When young this shrub is of erect growth, but later it becomes open and arching and reaches a height of about 2 m (6½ ft). The soft young shoots are reddish, covered with thorns and very decorative. Older stems are light brown with grey thorns. The single pale carmine flowers open in succession for three to four weeks beginning in about the first week of June and have a delicate fragrance. The light red elongate hips are very decorative.

R. x *highdownensis* is very resistant to frost and a healthy grower. This outstanding rose is not as widely used in landscape schemes as it deserves to be.

ROSA HUGONIS HEMSLEY   S.

True species, brought to Europe from central China in 1899

This is a vigorous, spreading shrub, the ratio of width to
height being 2.5 : 1.8 m (8 : 6 ft). The long shoots are
brownish-red and very prickly, arching at the tip in old
shrubs. The beautiful and luxuriant foliage is rather fern-
like; the individual leaves are about 8 cm ($3\frac{1}{4}$ in) long but
bear up to thirteen leaflets. From mid-May the whole bush is
covered with innumerable sulphur-yellow flowers. These are
single, 5 cm (2 in) across and without fragrance. Flowering
is not repeated. The hips are small, only about 1 cm ($\frac{1}{2}$ in)
long, ripening at the end of summer and falling very soon.

This rose is a must in large landscape schemes because of
its very early flowering and the wealth and glowing colour of
the blooms.

It belongs to the subgroup Pimpinellifoliae and has the
synonym *R. xanthina* CRÉPIN. It is sometimes known to gardeners as the Father or Père Hugo Rose and the Golden Rose of
China.

ROSA x HUGOPTERA

B. KAVKA, 1964; *R. hugonis* x *R. sericea pteracantha*

This is a very vigorous shrub, 3.5 m (about 4 yd) wide and 2.5 m (8 ft) high. The long robust shoots arch slightly with age and have a scattering of broad winged thorns inherited from *R. sericea pteracantha*. The flowers are somewhat smaller and paler in colour than those of the other parent *R. hugonis*. They bloom for seven weeks beginning in about the middle of May. The round hips are comparatively small, with a fleshy growth at the base. They fall at the end of summer as soon as they are ripe.

R. x *hugoptera* is a good rose for large landscape schemes. It looks most effective planted as a solitaire against a background of conifers.

ROSA MOYESII HEMSLEY and WILSON   S.

True species from western China, grown in Europe since 1894

This is a very vigorous, comparatively slender shrub of loose
habit; under favourable conditions it can grow to a height of
4 m (13 ft). The strong shoots are covered with large thorns.
The first velvety blood-red single flowers, 4 cm ($1\frac{1}{2}$ in) across,
appear at the beginning of June, followed in autumn by
large, bottle-shaped, light red hips, which — growing in
trusses of three to five — are very striking.

In addition to selected roses and hybrids the original wild
species *R. moyesii* is still used in landscape schemes, but mostly
in large parks in groups of mixed shrubs, and in rose collections (rosaria).

This rose belongs to the subgroup Cinnamomeae and is
also known under the synonyms *R. macrophylla rubrostaminea*
VILMORIN and *R. fargesii* OSBORN.

ROSA CENTIFOLIA MUSCOSA   S.

(AITON) SÉRINGE

The origin of this rose is not clear; it has been grown in Holland since 1720

Translated, the name *R. centifolia muscosa* means hundred-leaved moss rose, referring to the large number of petals and the encrustations of hairs of moss-like appearance on the sepals and calyx, and its common name is Moss Rose.

This shrub, which grows to a height of 1.5 m (5 ft), is upright in youth but later rather spreading and somewhat untidy. The leaves are pale green, with five to seven leaflets. The soft shoots are greenish and prickly. The full, double flowers are white or pink; they bloom in early June and have a very distinct fragrance.

The Moss Rose is of great historical interest and fits in very naturally in such situations as alongside old cottages. It was greatly admired by the Victorians.

This rose belongs to the subgroup Gallicanae and has the synonym *R. muscosa* AITON.

ROSA MULTIFLORA THUNBERG S.

True species of eastern Asia, grown in Europe since 1868

R. multiflora is a native of China, Japan and Korea. It has a natural inclination to produce new forms. Nurseries, where the original wild species is used, have both very thorny and thornless forms.

The shrub is very vigorous with arching branches; fully grown shrubs measure about 4 m (3 yd) in width and 2.5 m (8 ft) in height. The small flowers grow in very large clusters and are pure white with distinctive golden yellow stamens and a pleasant fragrance. The coral red hips are very small, only about 0.5 cm ($\frac{1}{4}$ in) in diameter. The foliage is dark and glossy changing to orange red in the autumn.

It makes a good specimen shrub in landscape schemes.

R. multiflora belongs to the subgroup Synstylae and is known under the following synonyms: *R. thunbergii* TRATTINNICK; *R. linkii* DENHARDT; *R. polyantha* SIEBOLD and ZUCCARINI; *R. thyrsiflora* LEROY; *R. intermedia* CARIÈRE; *R. wichurae* K.KOCH; *R. microcarpa* hort.; *R. multiflora thunbergiana* THORY; *R. dawsoniana* ELLWANGER and BARRY; *R. franchetii paniculigera* (MAKINO) KOIDZUMI.

ROSA POMIFERA HERRMANN   S.

True species, cultivated since 1771

This rose grows wild in Europe and western Asia. It is of
very upright habit, 2 m (6½ ft) high at the most, and comes
into bloom at the beginning of June. The flowers, one to three
to a stem, are a deep pink. The hips are red, ovate or elongate, 2—3 cm (¾—1¼ in) across and slightly bristly, and are
used in making rose hip syrup. The content of ascorbic acid
in the hips varies greatly in the different types. The foliage
is leathery, matt grey to metal-green.

The Apple Rose, as it is sometimes called, is valued in
landscape schemes more for its abundant display of red hips
than for its flowers and it is, therefore, recommended only for
large landscape schemes in combination with other shrubs.

It belongs to the subgroup Caninae and has the synonyms
R. villosa L. and *R. hispida* POIRET.

ROSA DAMASCENA MILLER   S.

Believed to be a true species, cultivated in Europe probably since
the sixteenth century

Rosa damascena, the Damask Rose, is believed to have originated in Asia Minor. According to unverified reports it is said
to have been first introduced into Europe in 1270 by the
Count de Brie, who brought it back to France. According to
Darlington, the cytologist, not only the French Rose *(R. gallica)* but also the Musk Rose *(R. moschata* HERRM*)* had a part
in the creation of the Damask Rose. *R. damascena* is a very
variable species, which also includes forms that are a source
of attar of roses.

The shrub reaches a height of 1.5—3 m (5—10 ft). The
flowers are double, very fragrant, and can be red, pink,
white or striped. As a rule they grow in trusses of several
blooms.

It is used in landscape schemes in the same way as *R. pomifera*.

R. damascena belongs to the subgroup Gallicanae and is also
known under the following synonyms: *R. calendarum* BORK-
HAUSEN; *R. polyanthos* ROESSIG; *R. belgica* MILLER; *R. gallica
damascena* VOSS.

ROSA SETIPODA HEMSLEY and WILSON

True species from central China, grown in Europe since 1895

A big shrub, attaining a height of 3 m (10 ft). The shoots ar
very vigorous and covered with large thorns. The single pa
pink flowers are 5 cm (2 in) across at the most, and are carrie
in loose clusters which begin to open at the end of June. Th
very long pear-shaped hips (3 cm; $1\frac{1}{4}$ in long) are dark re
and covered in fine bristles which extend down over the ster
(hence the name *setipoda* meaning bristly stem). The leave
are slightly fragrant.

Rosa setipoda is effective grown in solitary groups in larg
landscape schemes. The autumn colouring of the leaves i
very decorative and attractive.

It belongs to the subgroup Cinnamomea and is also known
as *R. macrophylla crasseaculeata* VILMORIN.

This is a very vigorous, thick shrub with few thorns and rather pendulous growth. The single flowers, borne in early June, are pale pink. The hips are round-ovate, pale red, and ripen very late. The seeds should be stratified before sowing.

Similar rootstock roses are *R. canina* 'Brög's' with a growing period even longer than that of *R. canina inermis*, and *R. canina* 'Schmidt's Ideal', which is the most vigorous and thorny-stemmed of the three. All these roses are subject to mildew. *R. canina inermis*, *R. canina* 'Brög's' and *R. canina* 'Schmidt's Ideal' are rootstock roses good for greenhouse cultivation or for outdoor cultivation in light soils. Together with *R. canina pollmeriana*, they belong to the subgroup Caninae.

ROSA CANINA POLLMERIANA R.

POLLMER 1904; *R. canina* L. x *R. setigera* MICHAUX

This is a plant of vigorous, upright habit with only the old stems arching slightly at the top. The coffee-red stems are practically without thorns. The single flowers are white. The hips are red, ovate, and ripen in late September. The leaves are regularly subject to black spot.

R. canina pollmeriana is the best rootstock for outdoor cultivation in heavy soils. It belongs to the subgroup Caninae.

ROSA x ODORATA (ANDREWS) SWEET R

Hybrid from R. chinensis x R. gigantea from western China

In Europe this rose was recorded in Upsala as early as 1752 and in Kew in 1769. At the present time it is used chiefly as a rootstock for hothouse roses.

The plant has a vigorous, loose growth, attaining a height of 3 m (10 ft). The foliage is a glossy, dark green. The flowers are semi-double, delicate pink and fragrant. In warmer climates R. x *odorata* can also be grown in mixed groups of shrubs in large landscape schemes.

This hybrid belongs to the subgroup Indicae and is also known under the following synonyms: R. *indica odorata* ANDREWS; R. *indica fragrans* THORY; R. *indica odoratissima* LINDLEY; R. *thea* SAVI; R. *chinensis fragrans* (THORY) REHDER; R. *gechouitangensis* LÉVEILLÉ; R. *oulengensis* LÉVEILLÉ; R. *tong-tchouanensis* LÉVEILLÉ. Nurserymen's terminology also includes the name R. *chinensis major*.

ROSA EGLANTERIA L.   R.

True species from Europe, cultivated since 1551

A slow-growing, compact shrub, this species attains a height
of 1.5 m (5 ft). The stems are short and covered with small
thorns. The small oval leaves are a glossy dark green with
a wine-like scent, which is why *R. eglanteria* is also known as
the Wine Rose. The single pink flowers are borne singly or in
groups of three to five on short stems. The flowering period
is in mid-June. The small red hips ripen in September.

R. eglanteria is a very good understock for miniature roses.

It belongs to the subgroup Caninae and is also known as
R. rubiginosa L; *R. suavifolia* LIGHTFOOT; *R. walpoleana* GREENE.

HIPS: Rosa rugosa THUNB.
Rosa multiflora THUNB.
Rosa canina L.

The size, shape and colour of the hips are often characteristic of a particular species or variety and an important means of identification, especially in the case of wild roses.

Rosa rugosa has flattened globular hips that are large and therefore conspicuous even at a distance. The sepals at the tips of the hips are ribbon-like and together with the glowing red of the fruit and autumn colouring of the rugose leaves create a very attractive and decorative effect. *R. rugosa* is also known as the Japanese Apple Rose.

Rosa multiflora has quite different hips. They are small, coral red, growing in an upright cluster and with practically no sepals. The hips of *R. helenae* REHD. and WILS. are of similar shape and colour but the clusters are not so full or so erect.

For the purpose of showing the great variety in hips those of the well-known Dog Rose (*Rosa canina* L.) are also included. In this connection, however, it is necessary to point out that many different forms of the Dog Rose are to be found growing wild and that their hips may differ in size, shade of red, size of the sepals, etc.

HIPS: *Rosa pomifera* HERRMANN
Rosa spinosissima L.
Rosa moyesii HEMSLEY and WILSON

The hips of *R. pomifera* look very much like apples and henc
the name Apple Rose. They are about as large as the hips o
R. rugosa but ovate rather than spherical and coloured ;
bright or dark red.

The hips of *R. spinosissima* are unique for unlike most hips
which are red or sometimes yellowish, they are glossy and
entirely black when ripe.

R. moyesii has hips that are of quite a different shape from
those already mentioned. They are elongate pear-shaped,
pale red, and grow in bunches of three to five. The fruits of
R. setipoda are similar to these hips and so are the large and
lovely hips of *R. sweginzowii* KOEHNE.

In an endeavour to acquaint the reader, at least in part,
with the great variety of colour and hip shape the fruits of six
true species which represent the main shapes are shown here.
Wild roses and certain shrub roses — as yet little 'unified' by
hybridization — have preserved the great variety of form and
colour of the hips and in the case of some simple hybrids such
as *R.* x *highdownensis* have even increased it.

LIST OF PLATES

234